This coloring book belongs to

. . . .

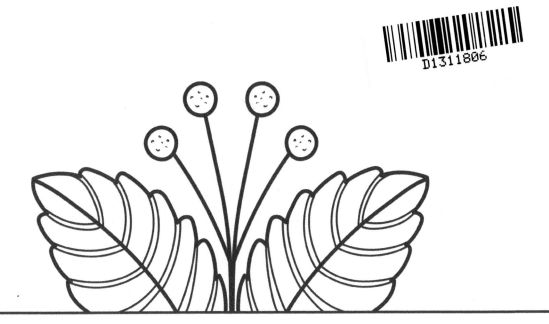

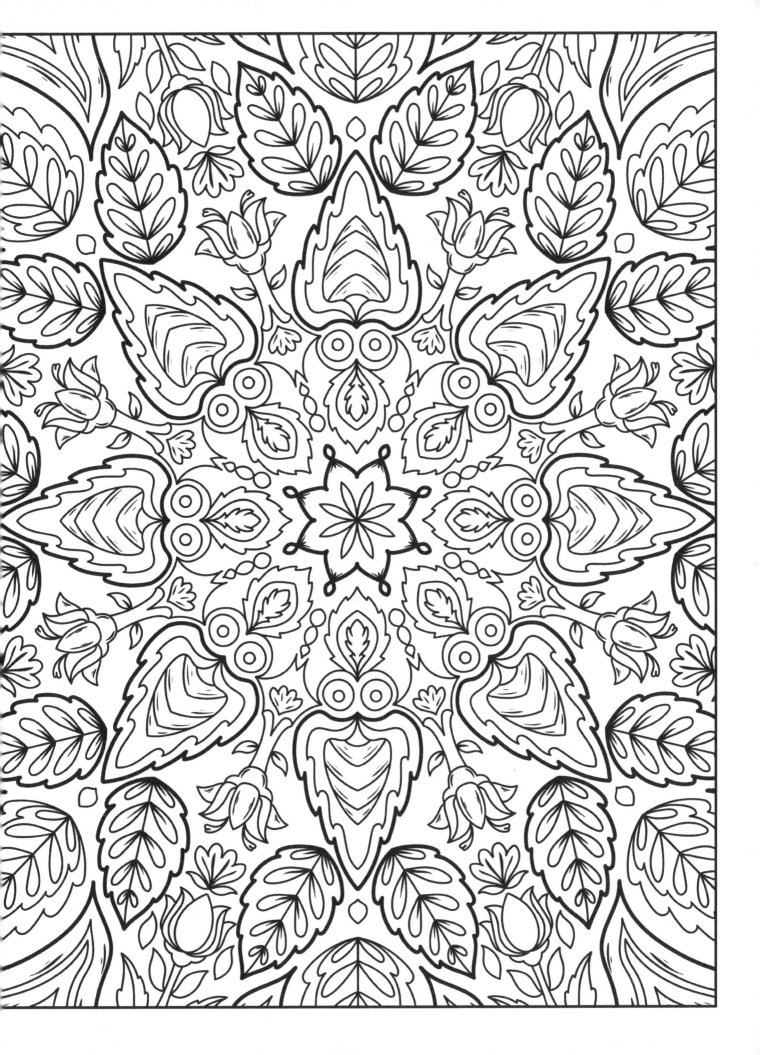

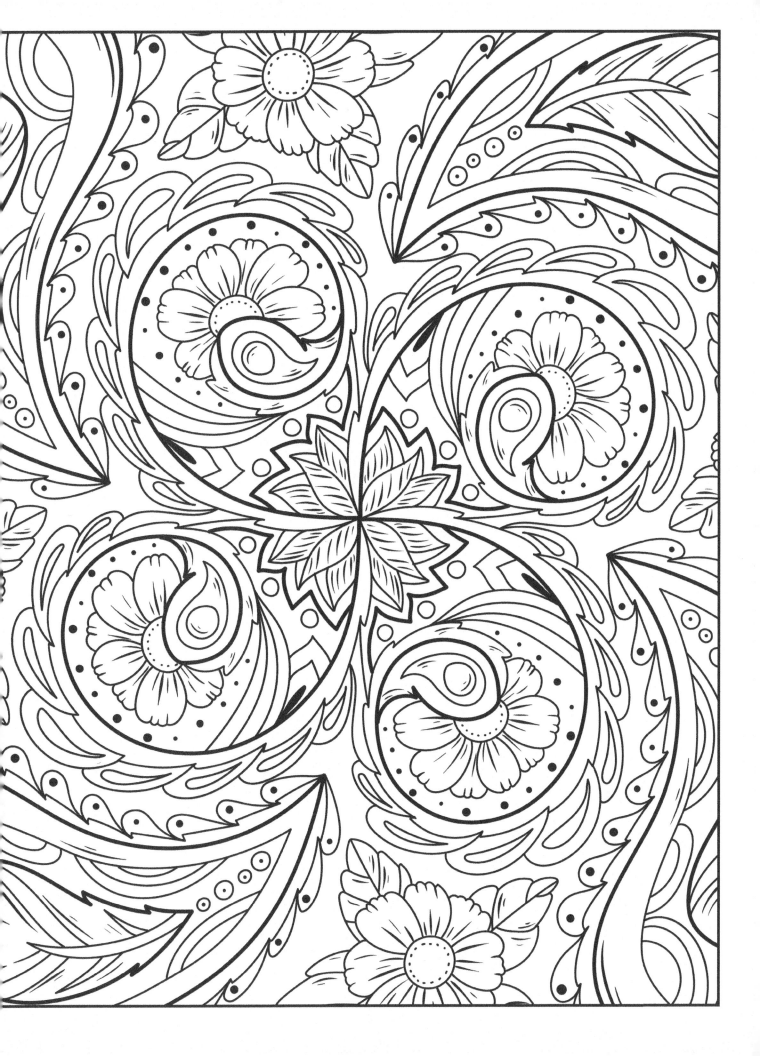

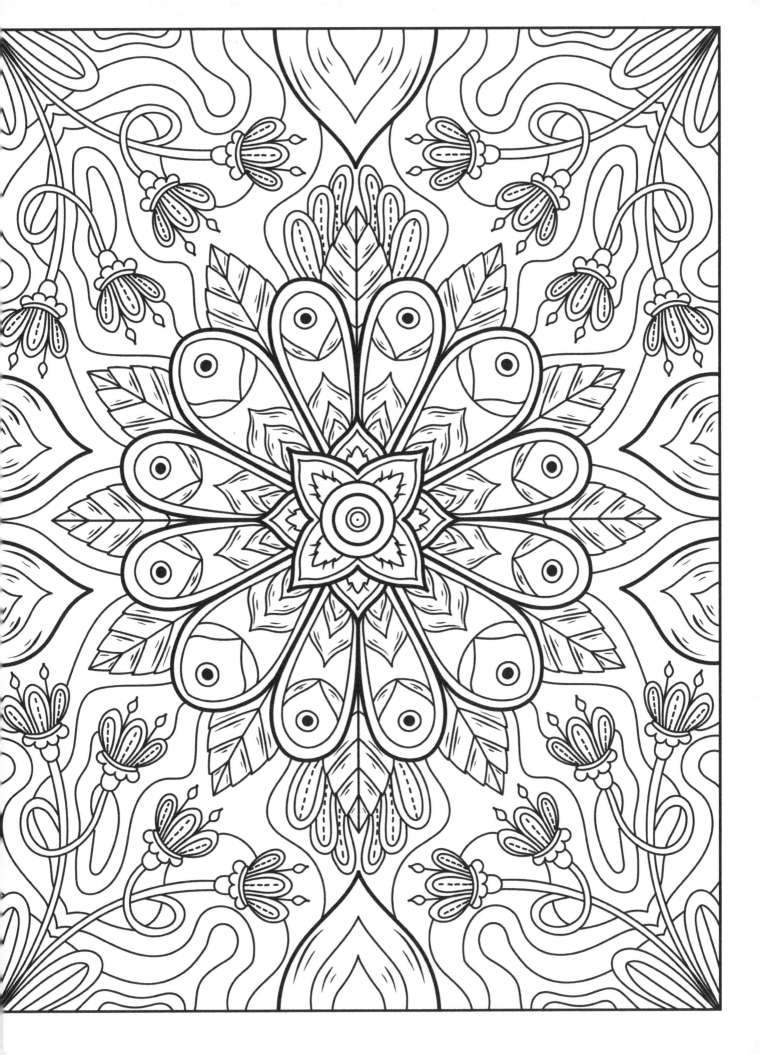

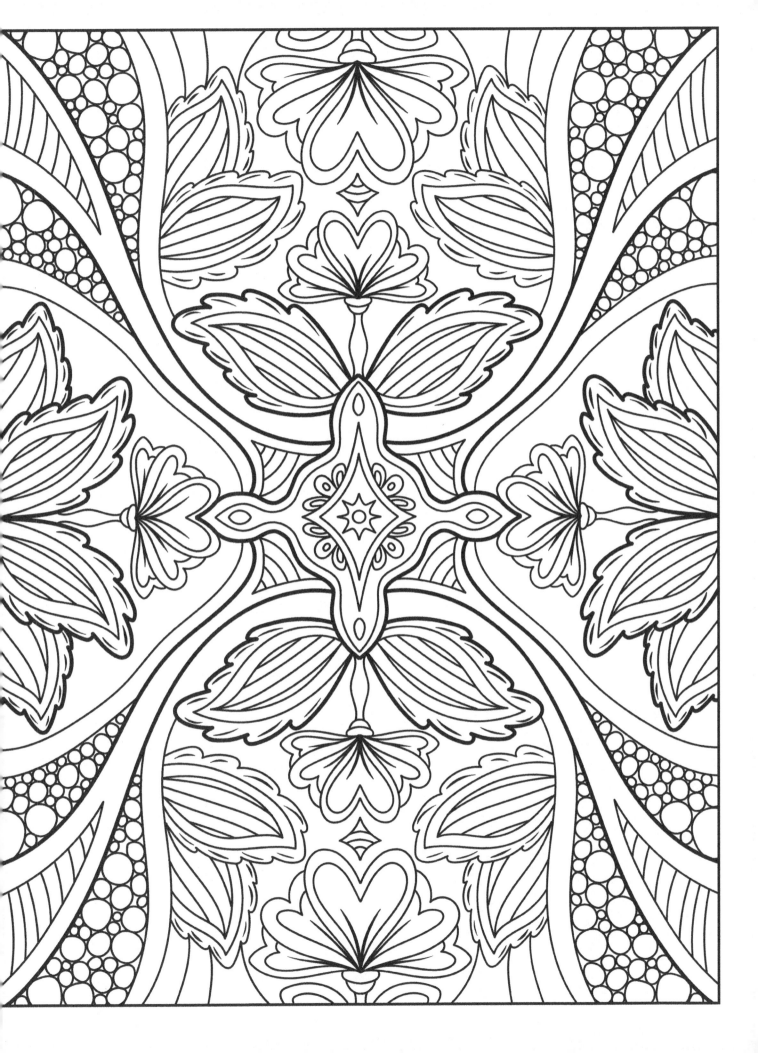

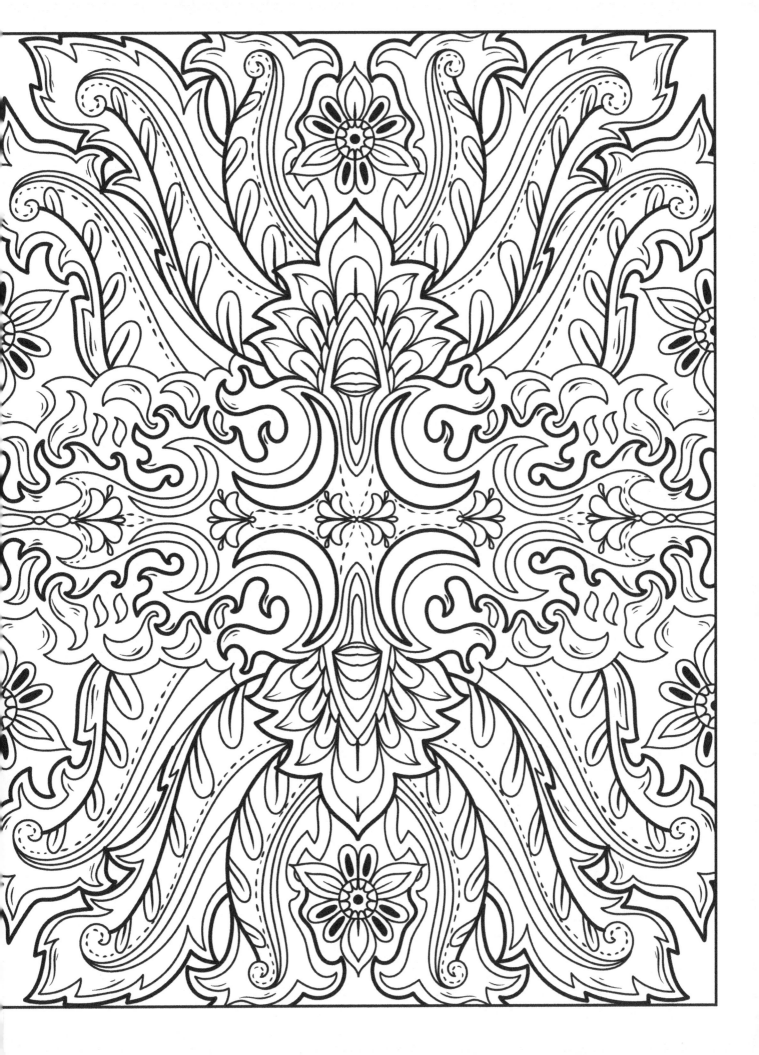

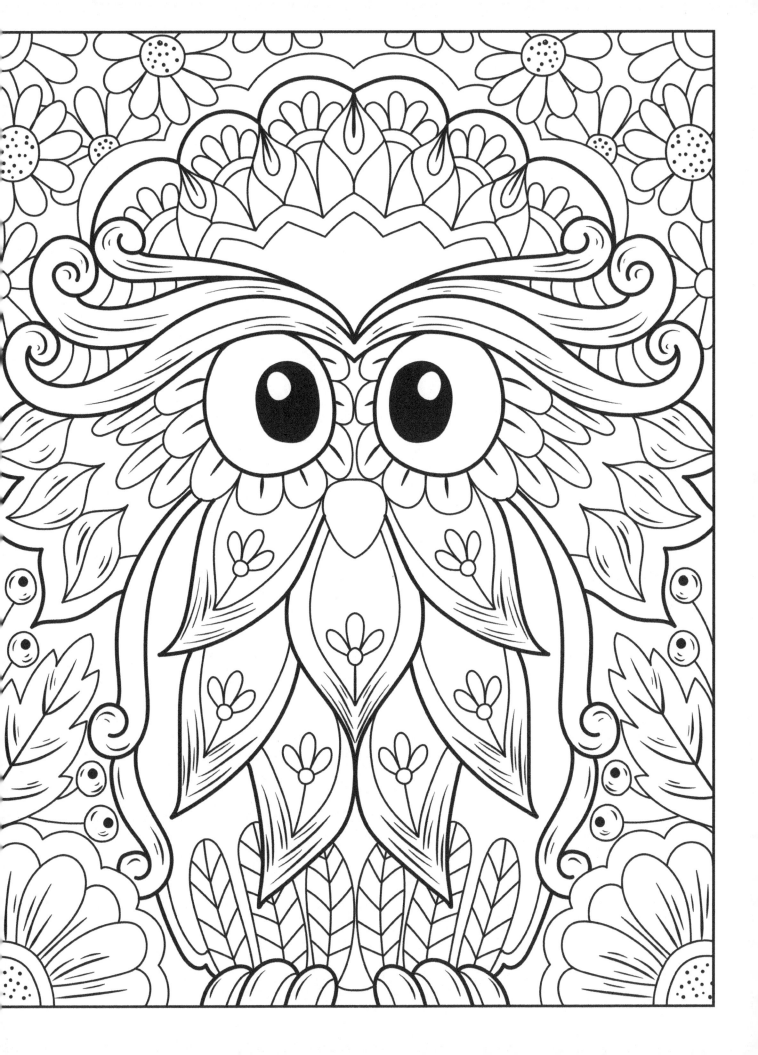

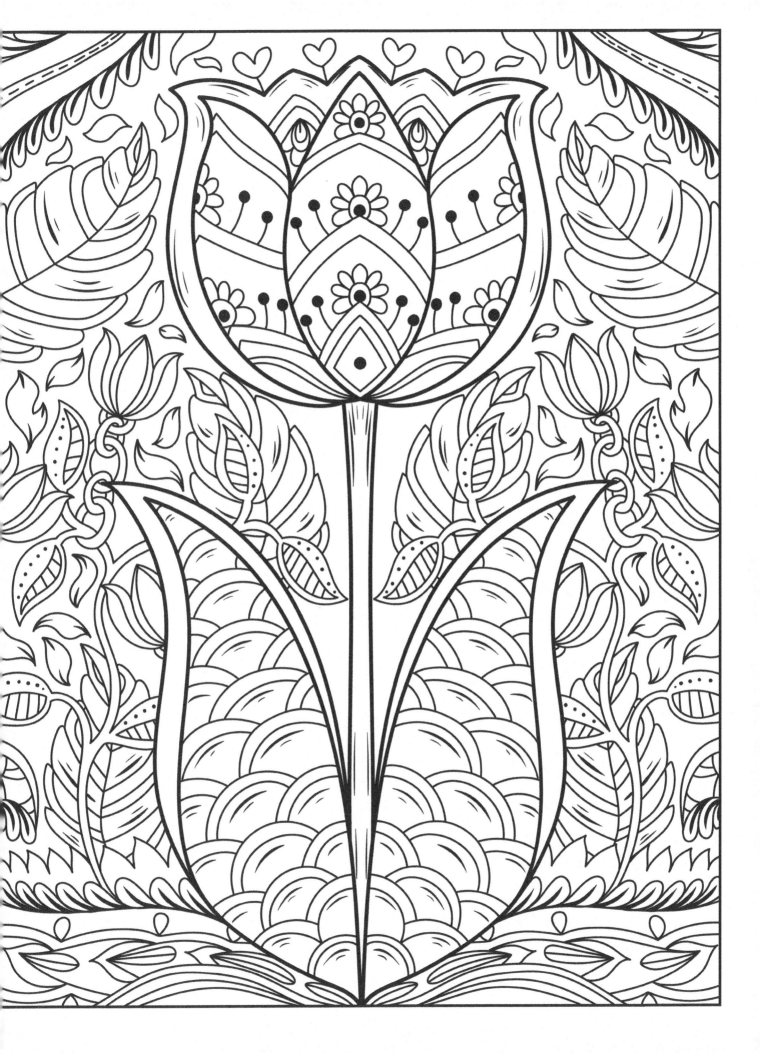

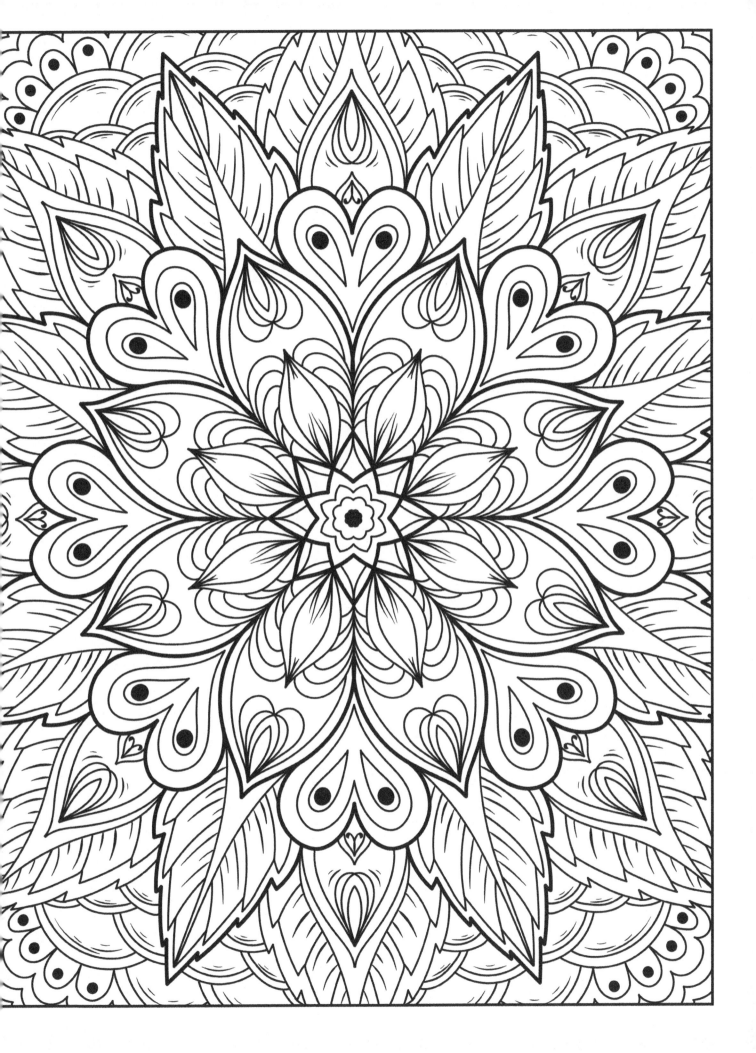

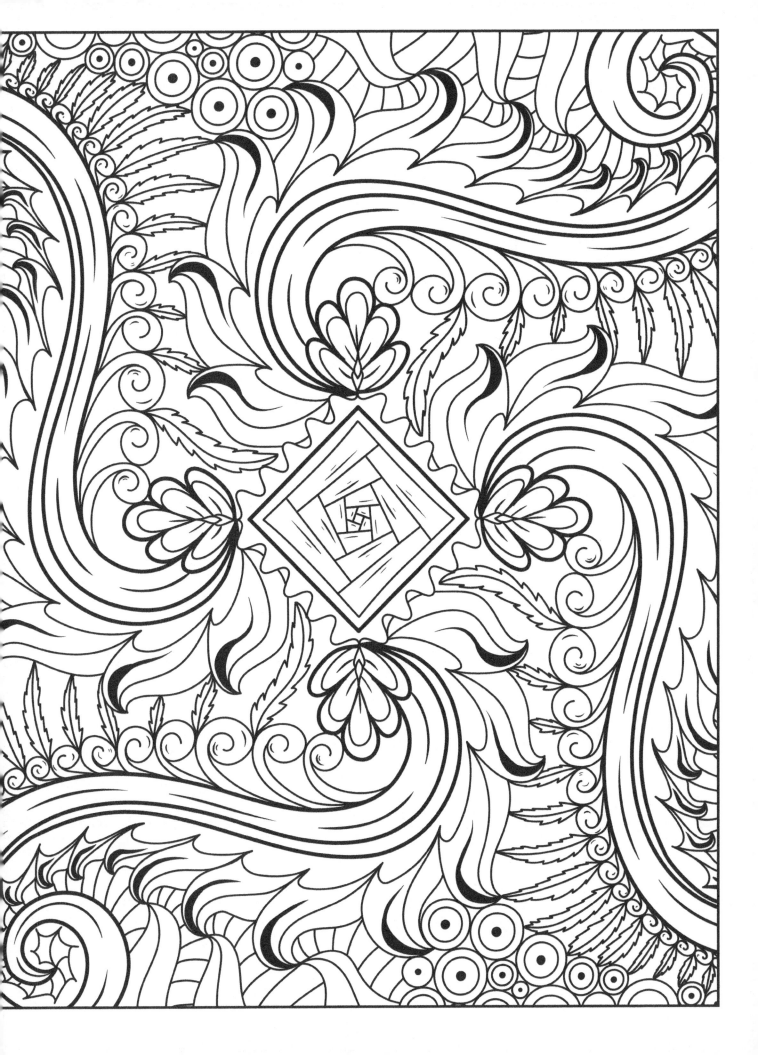

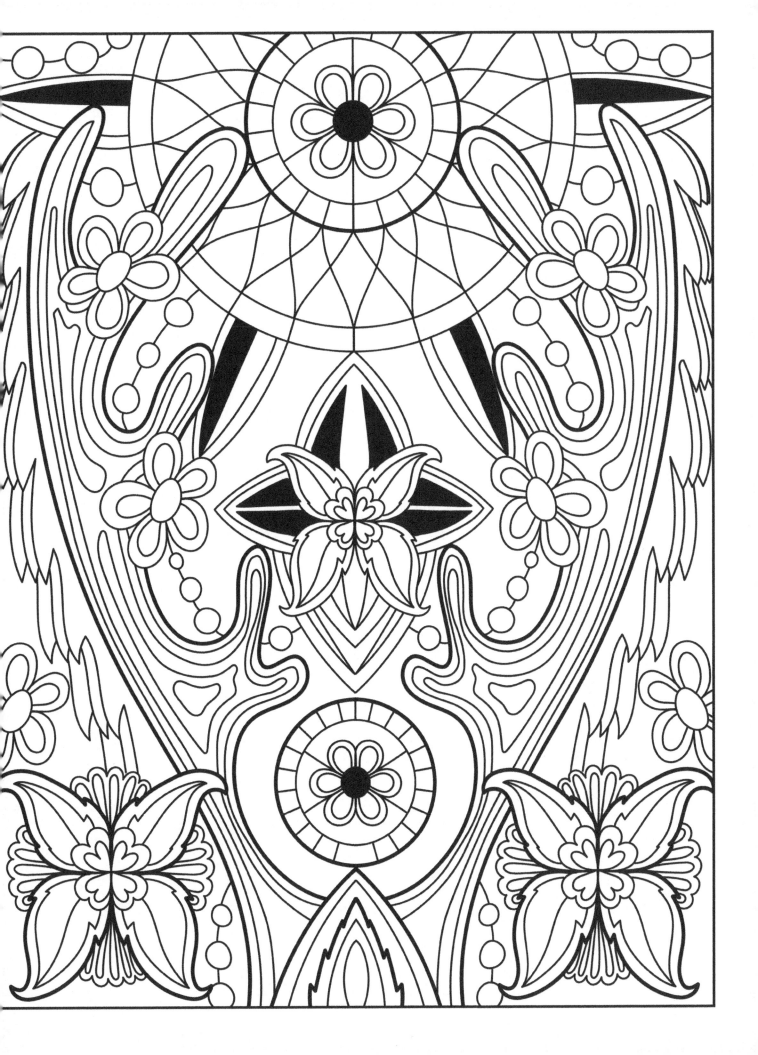

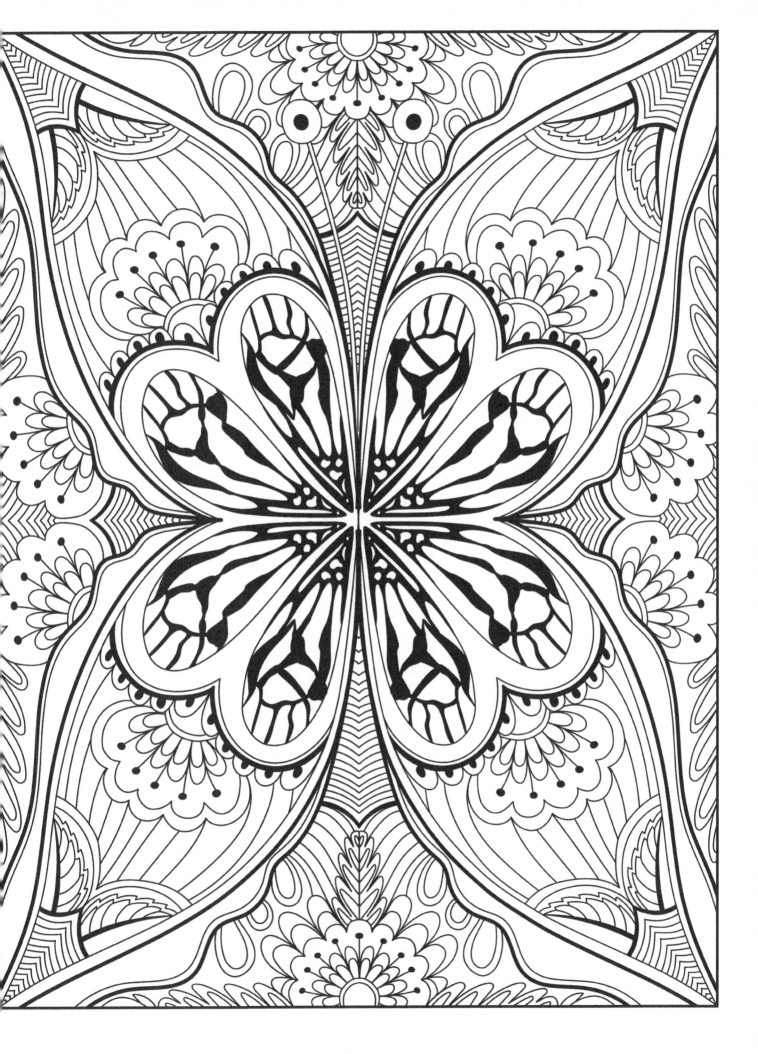

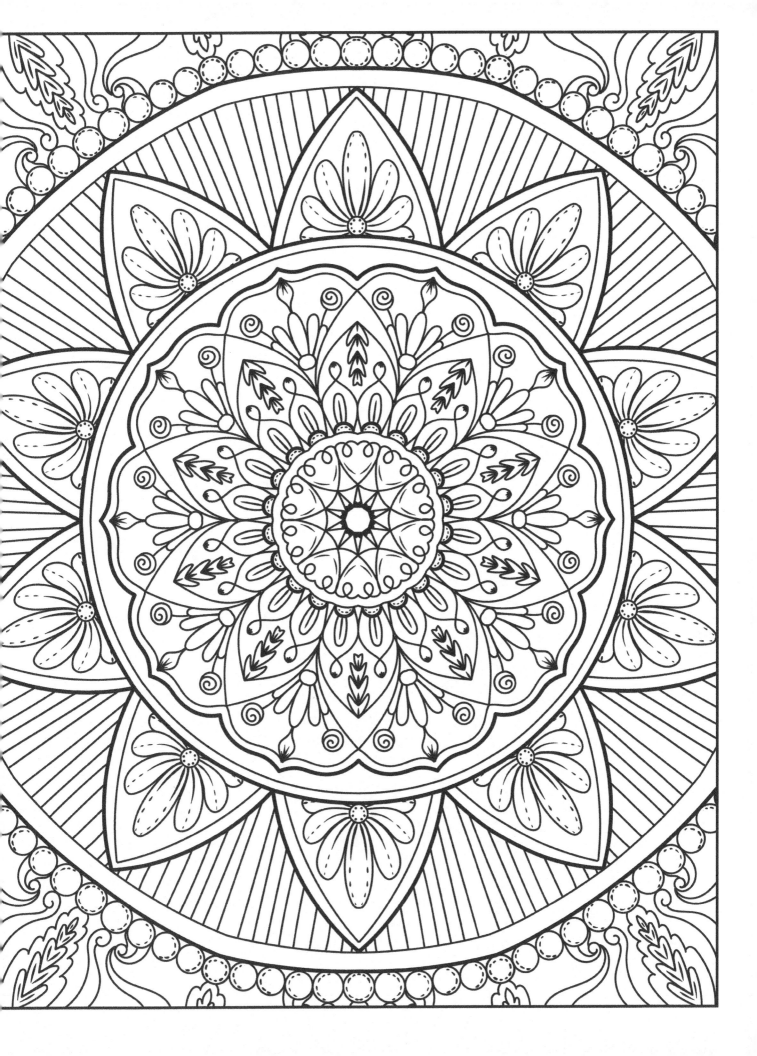

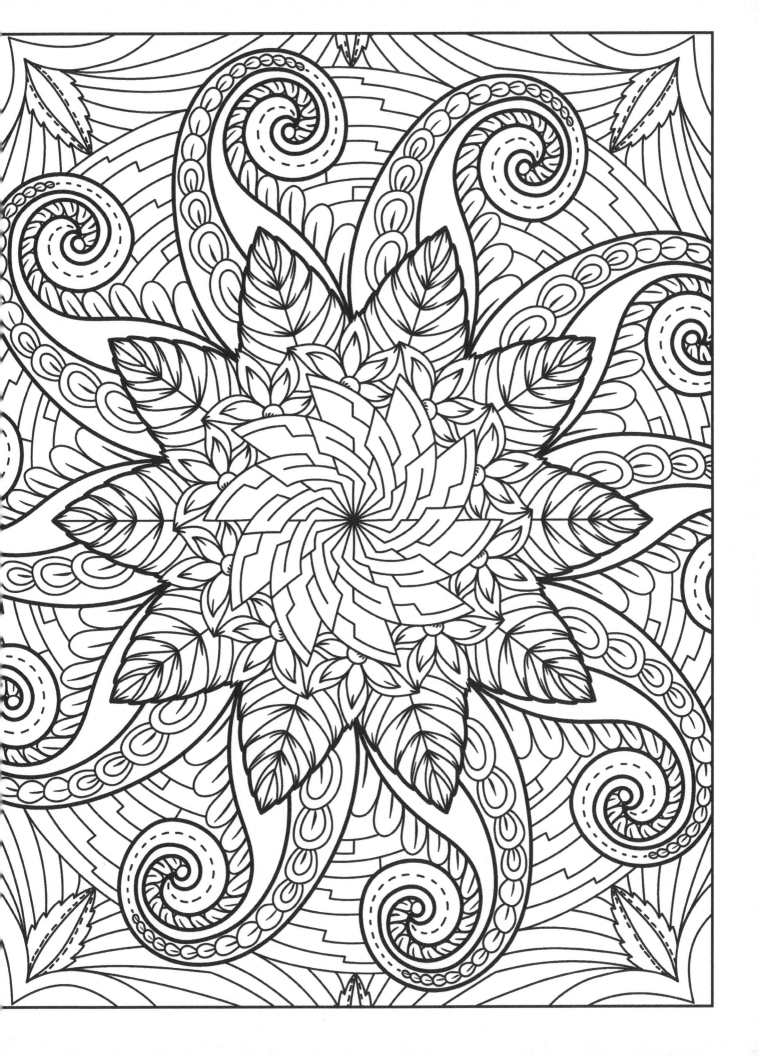

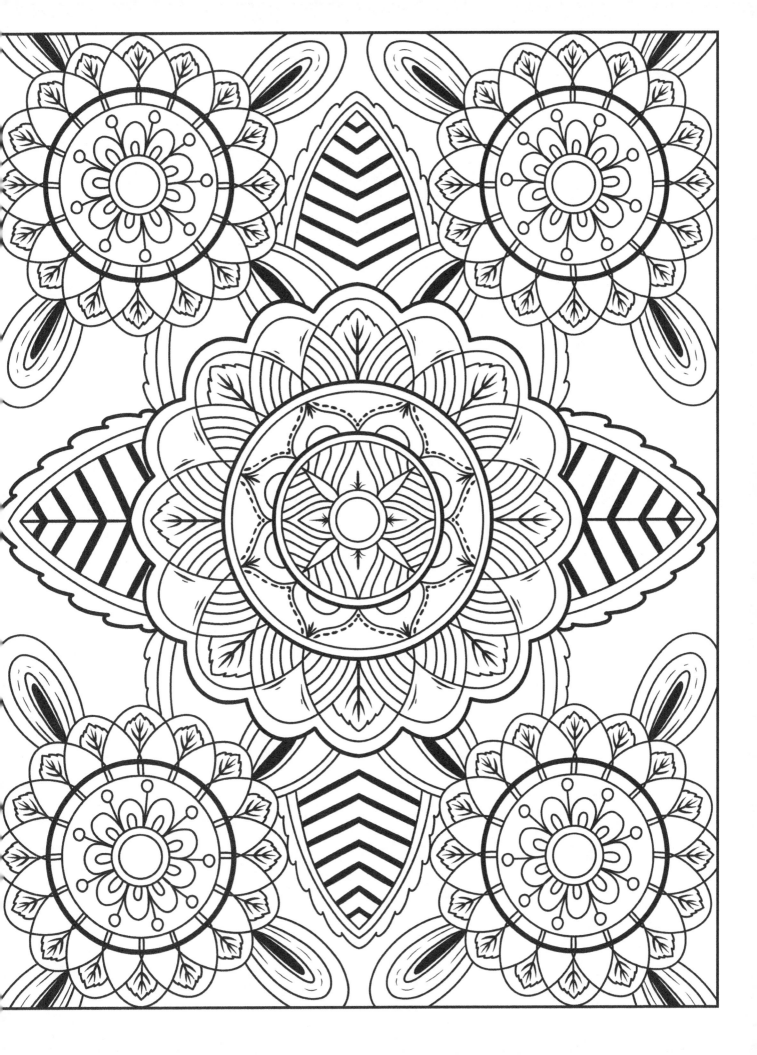

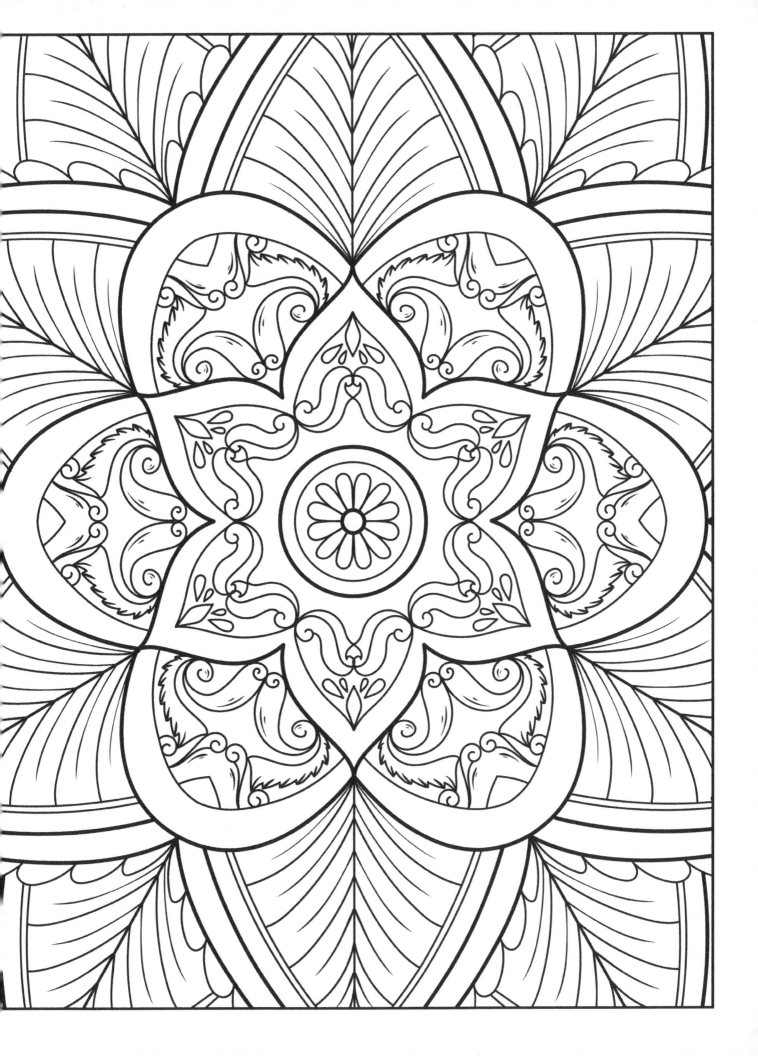

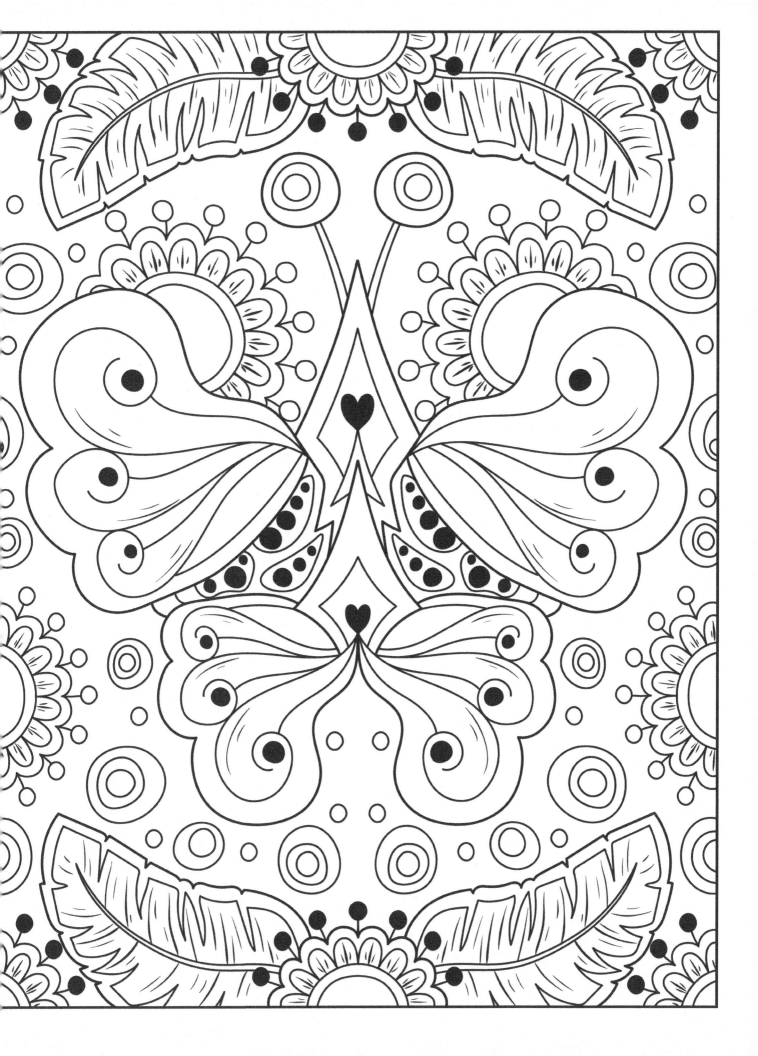

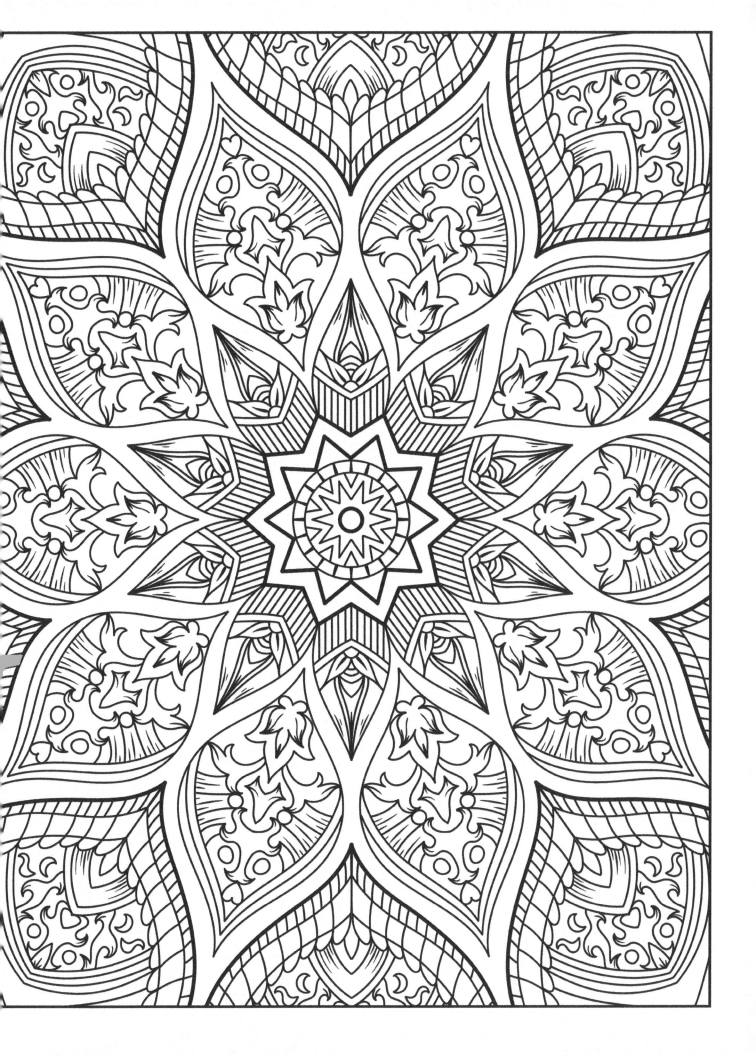

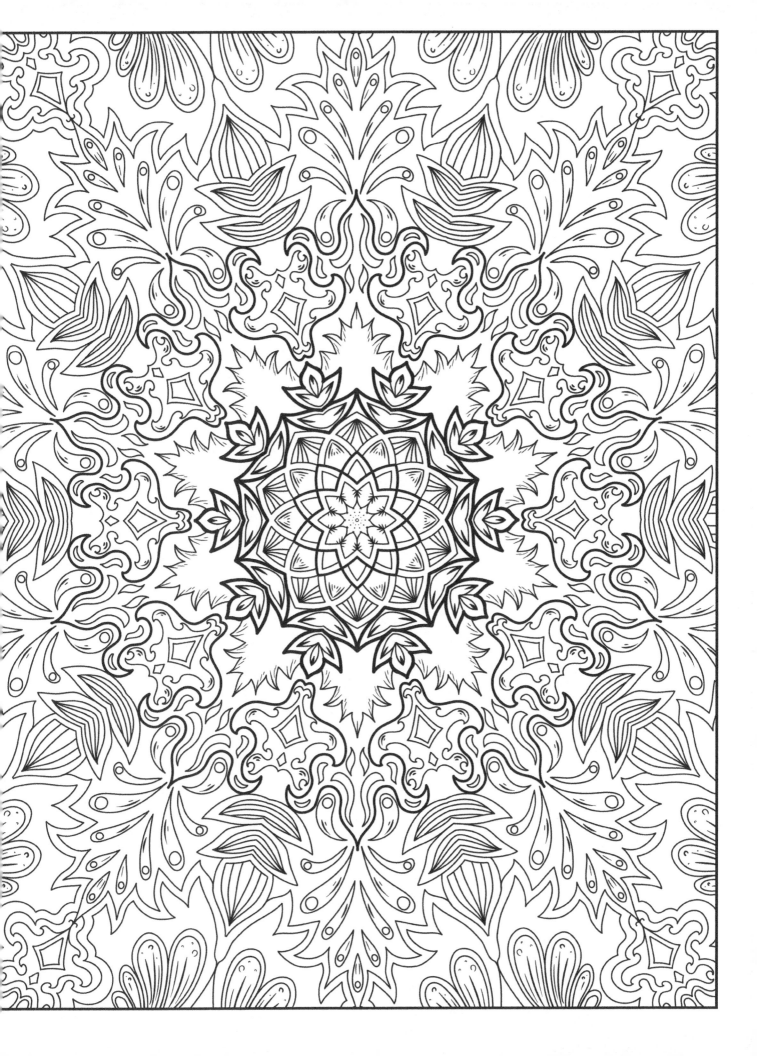

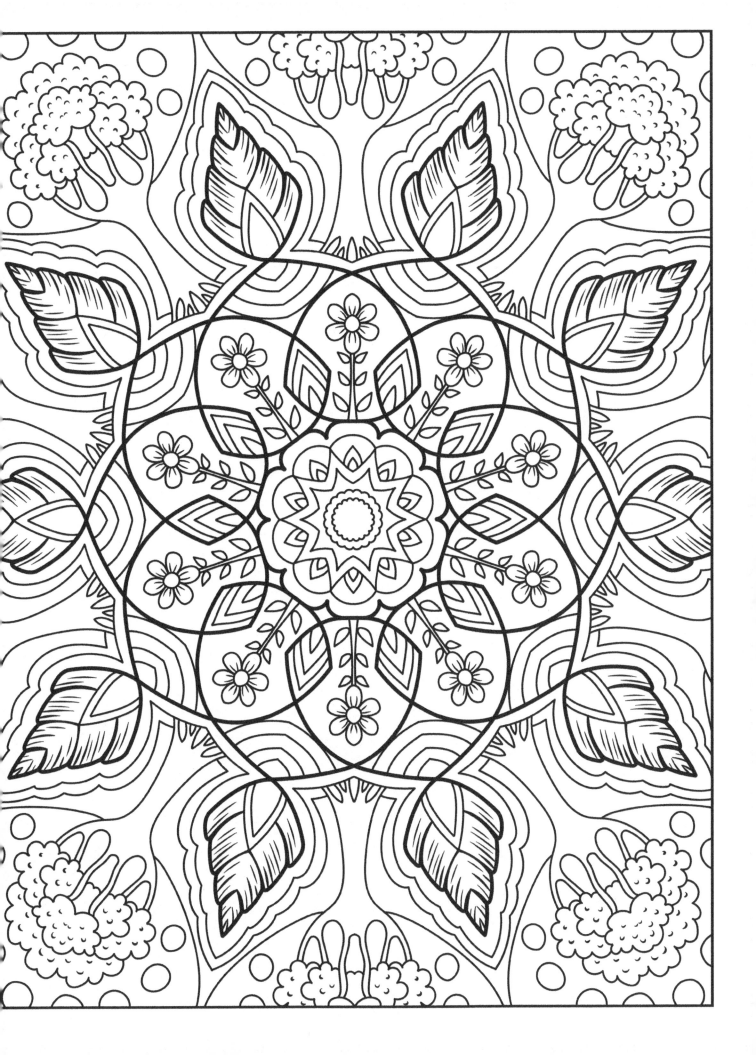

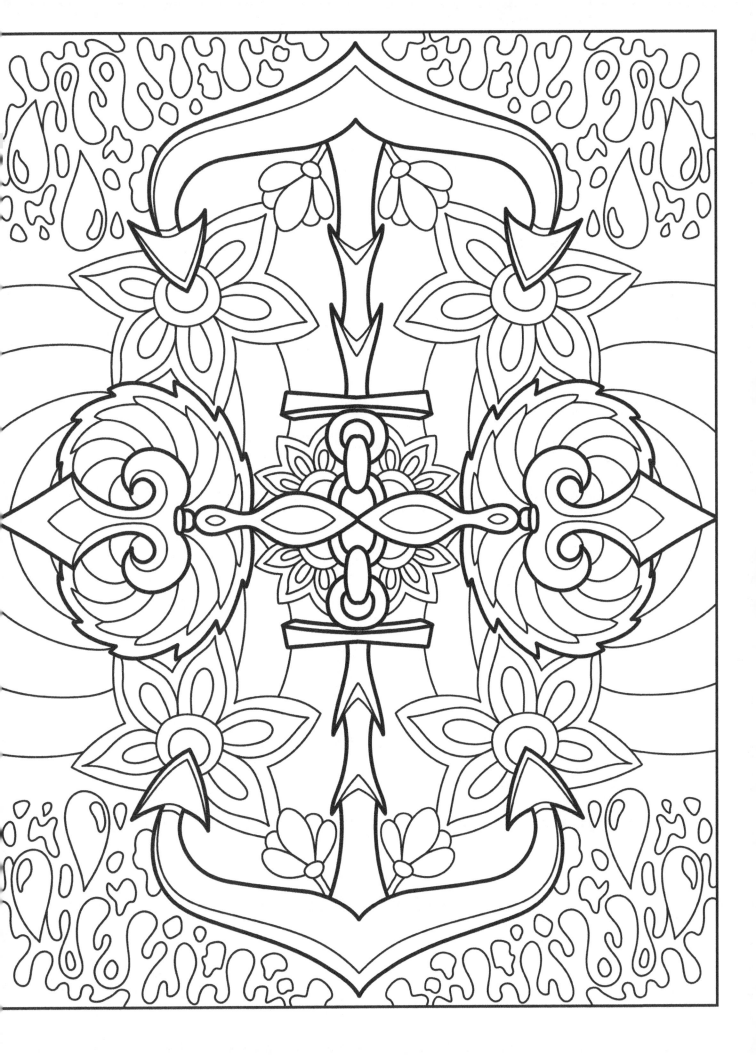

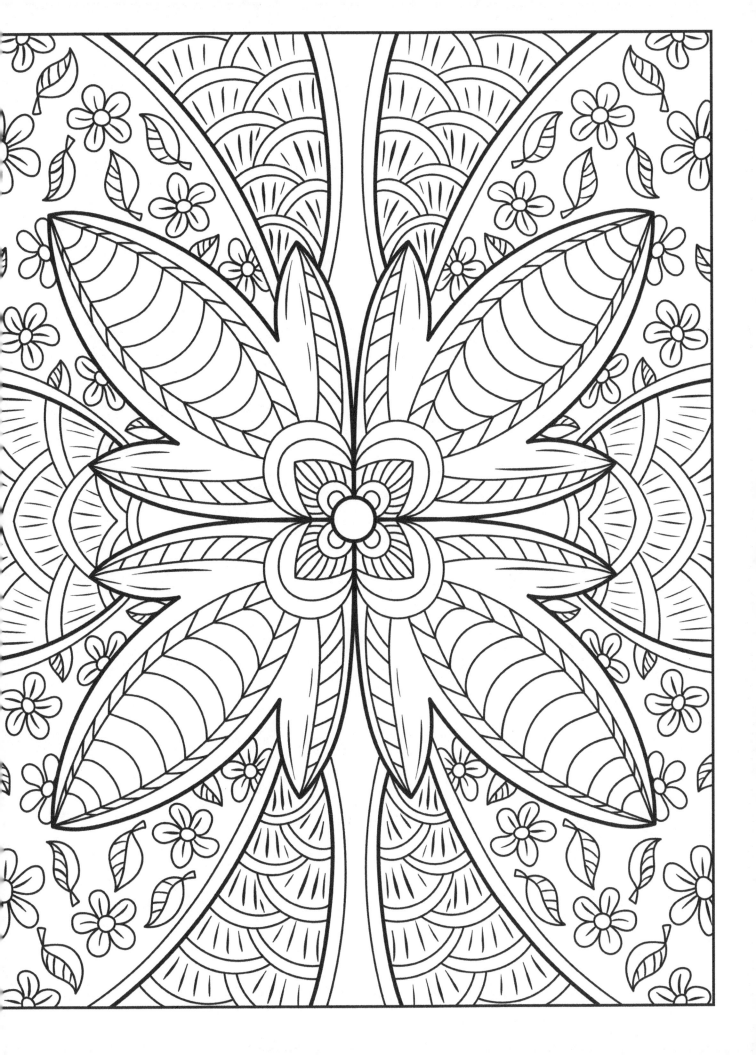

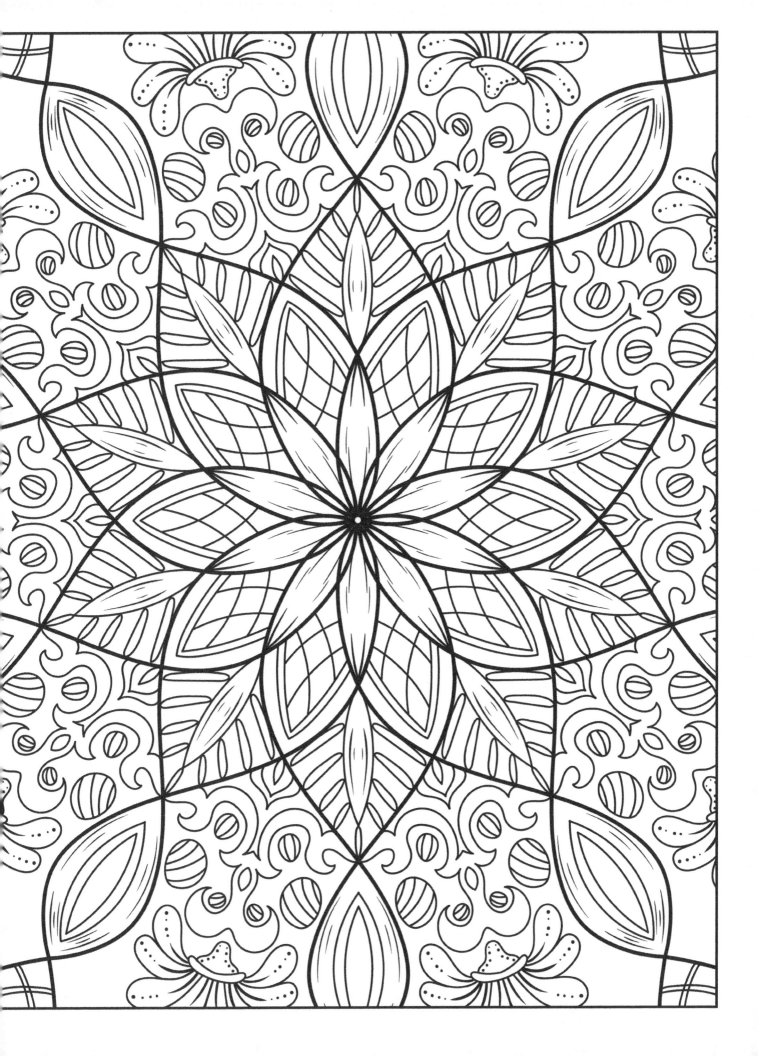

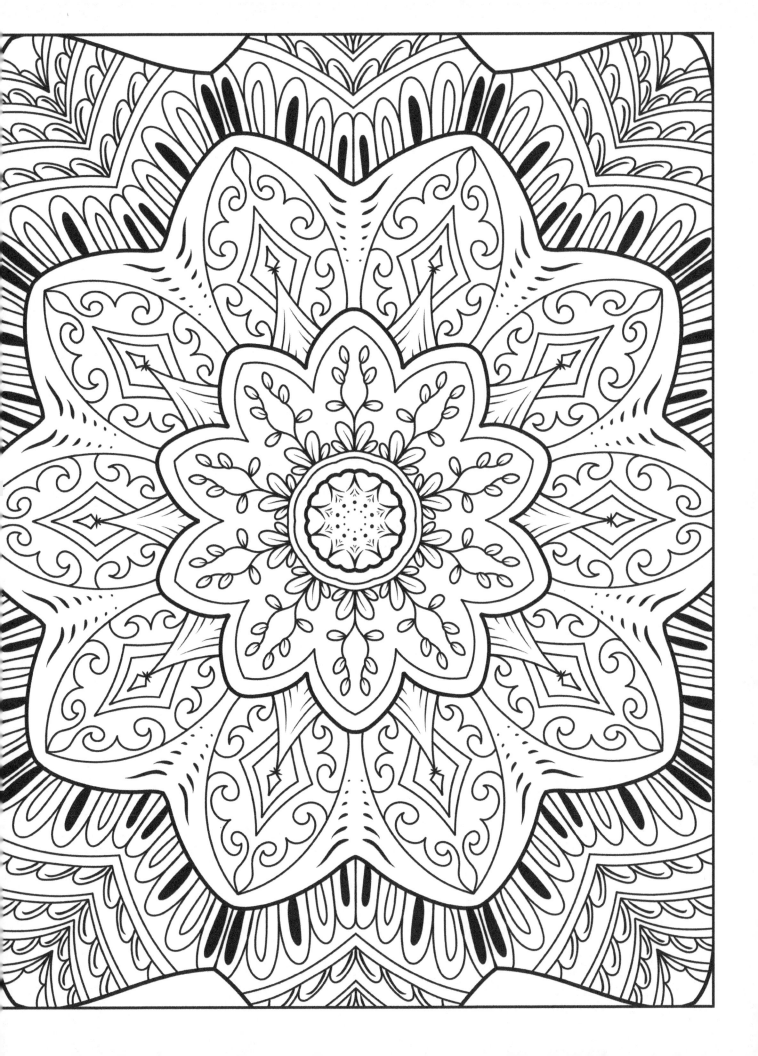

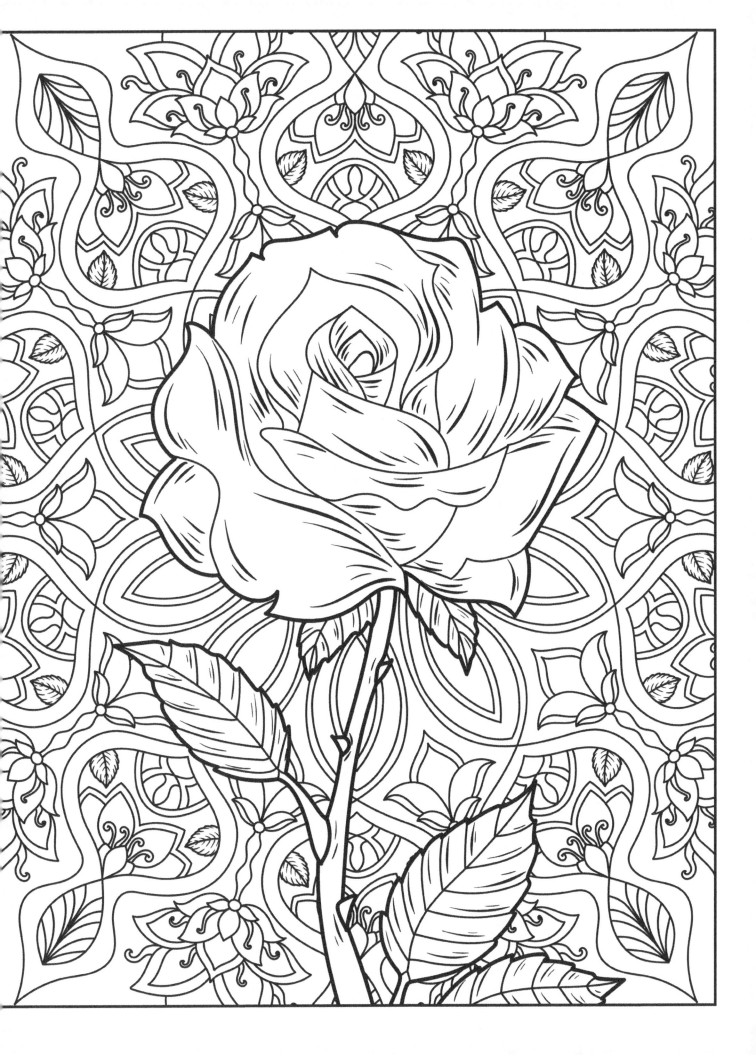

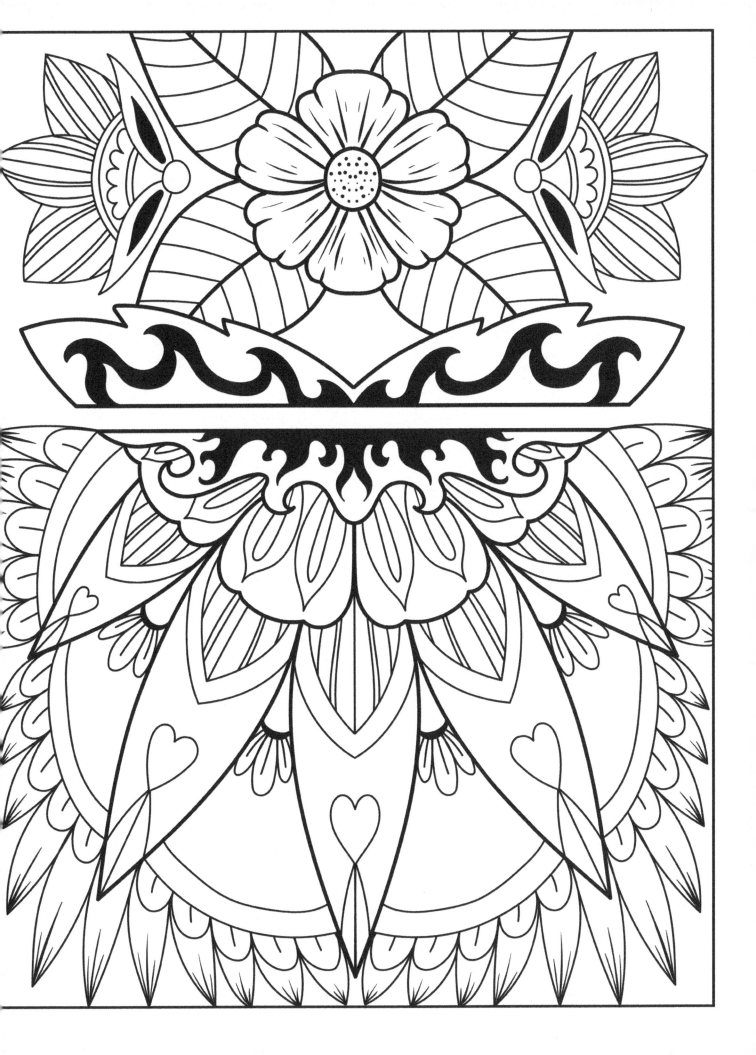

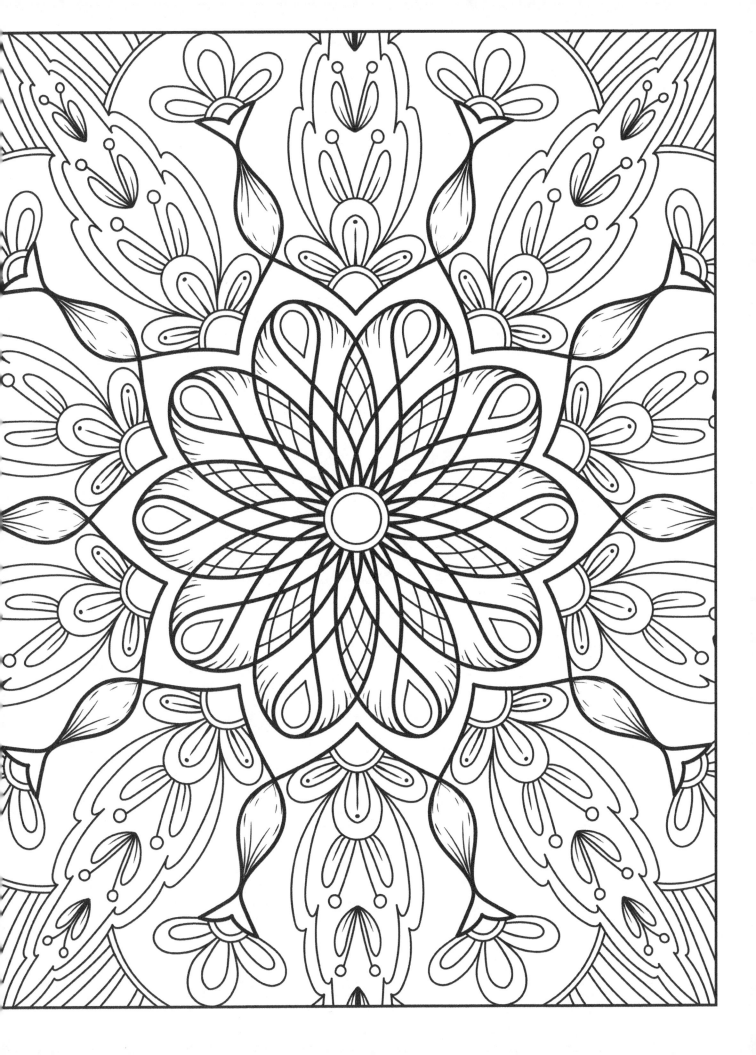

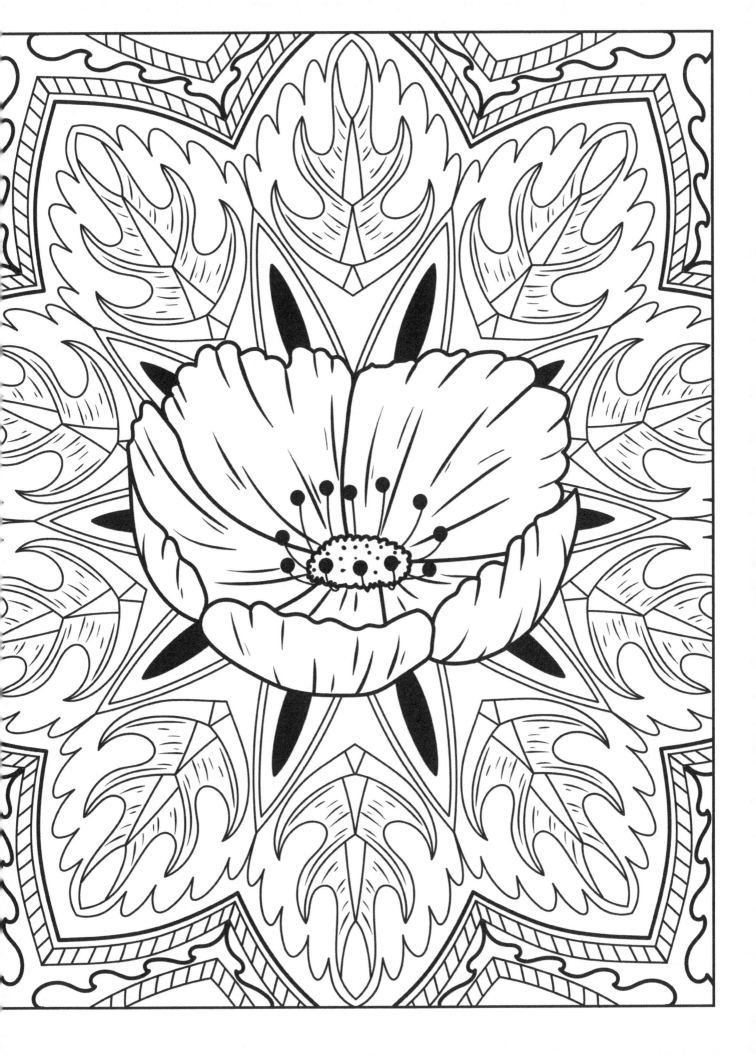

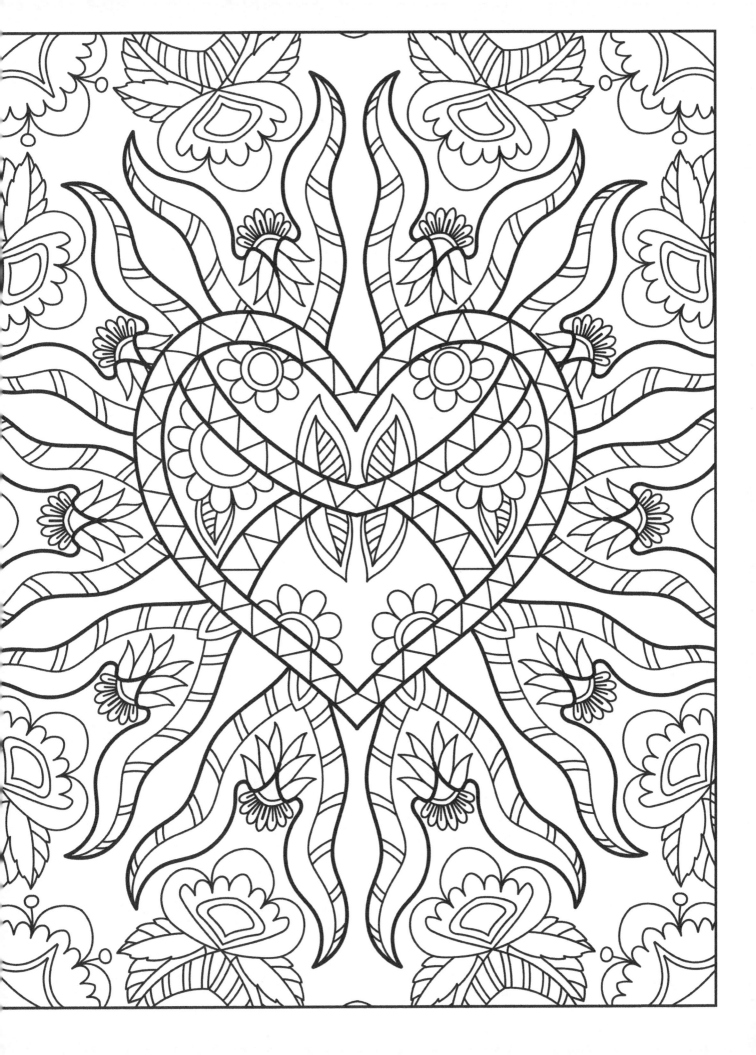

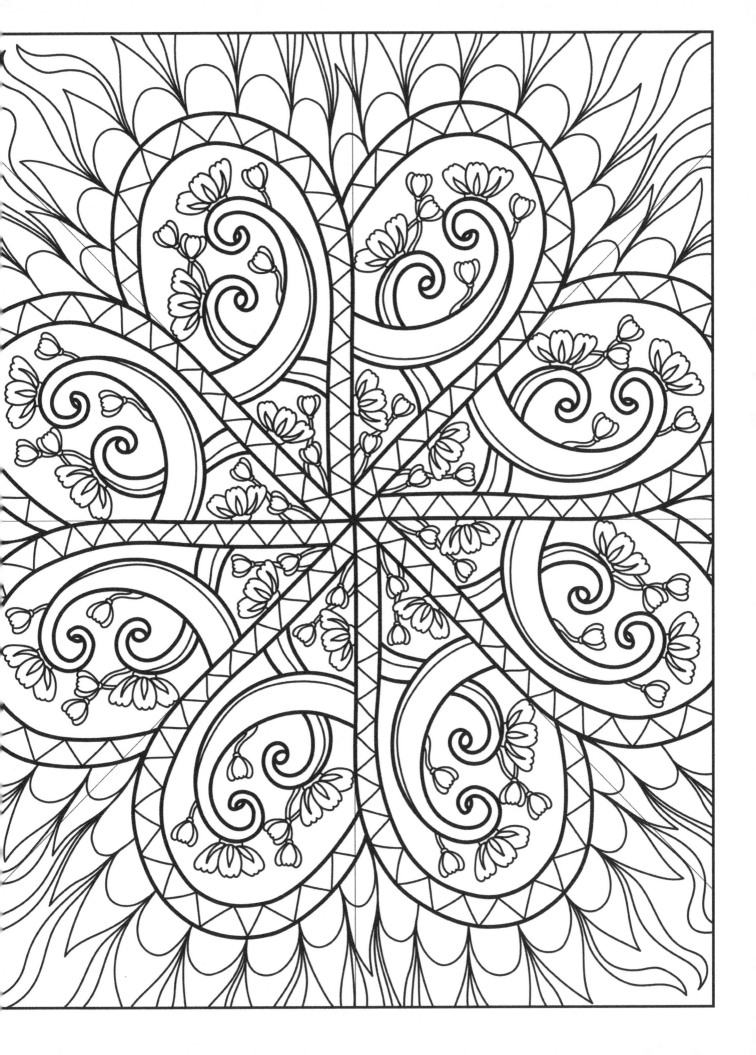

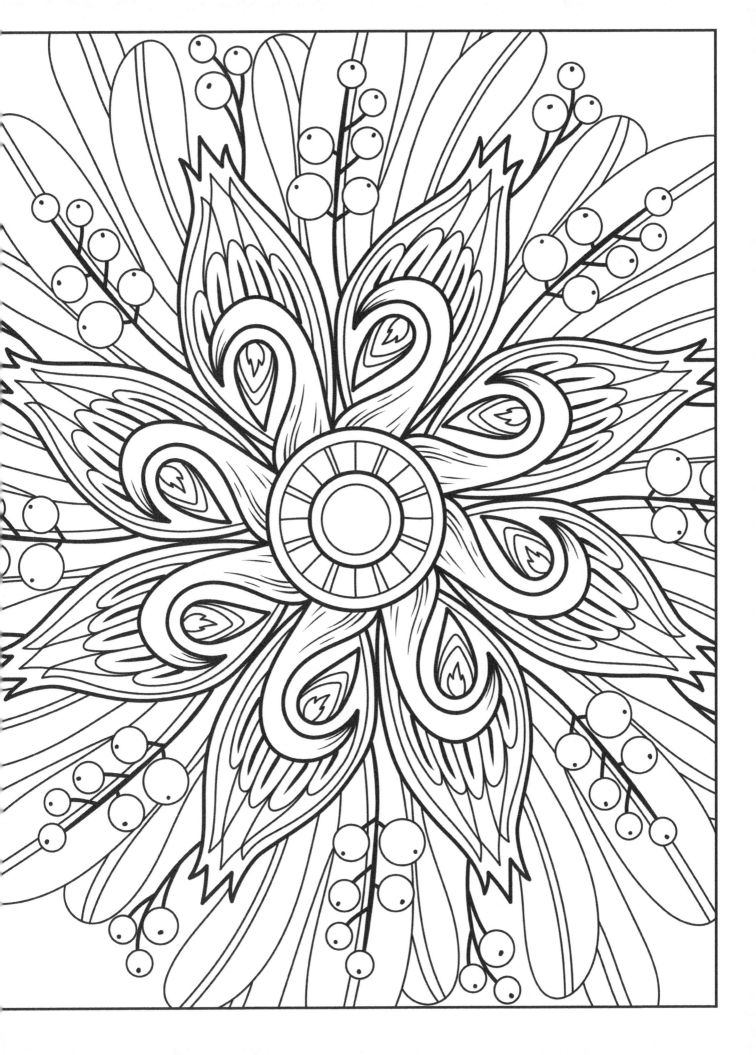

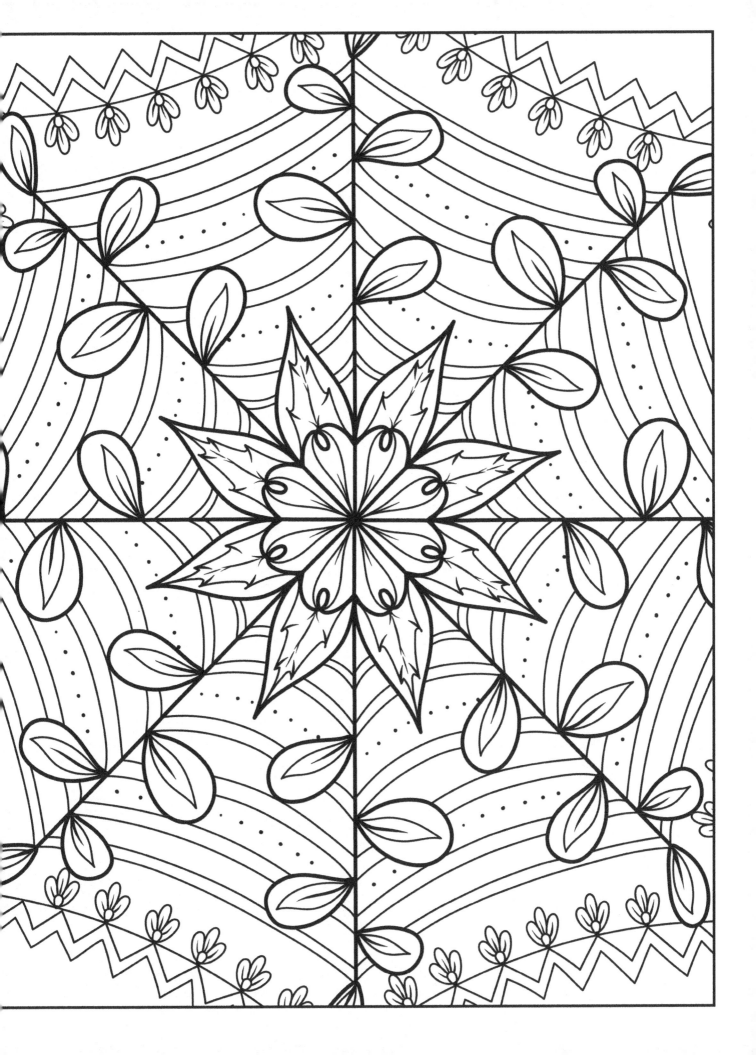

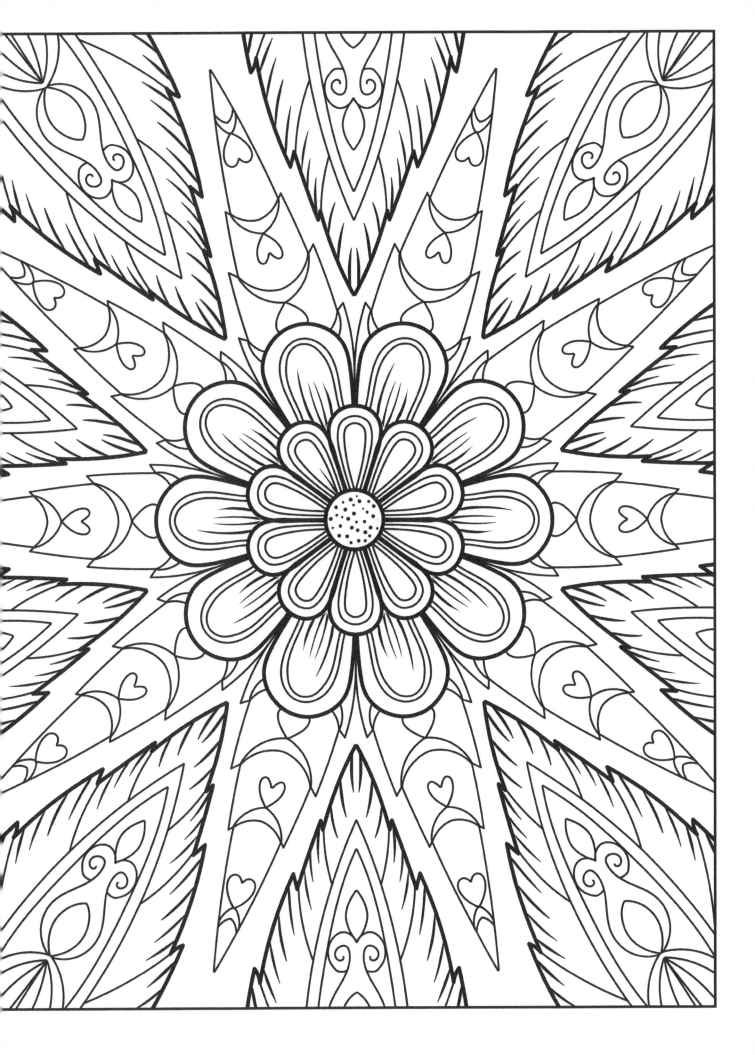

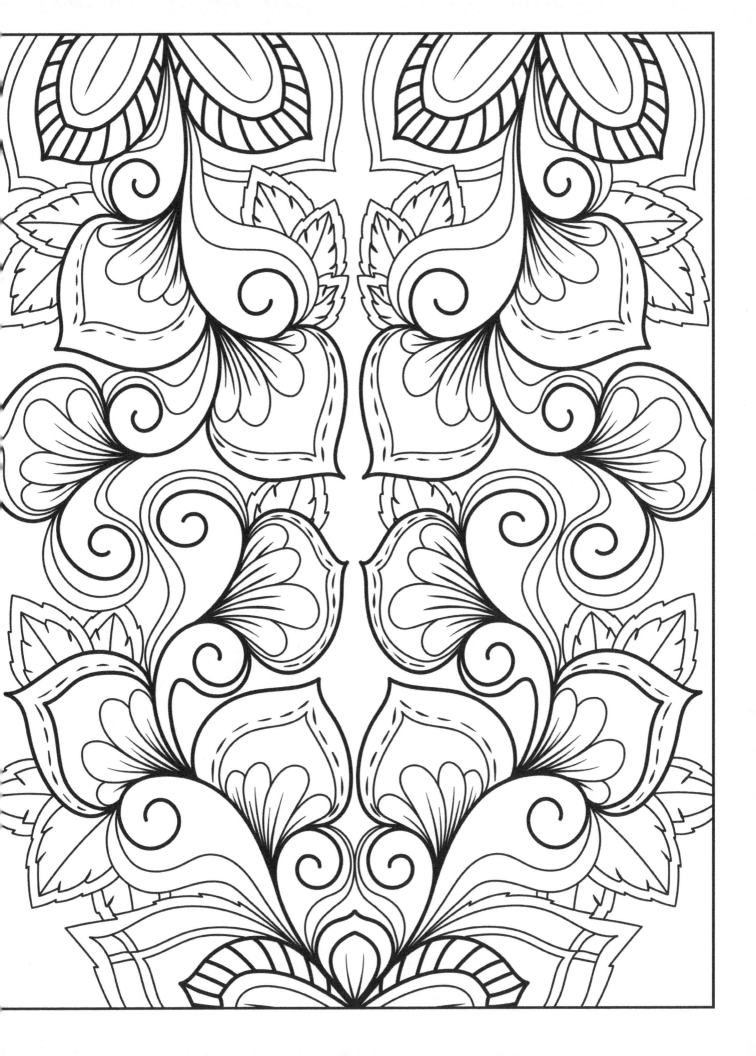

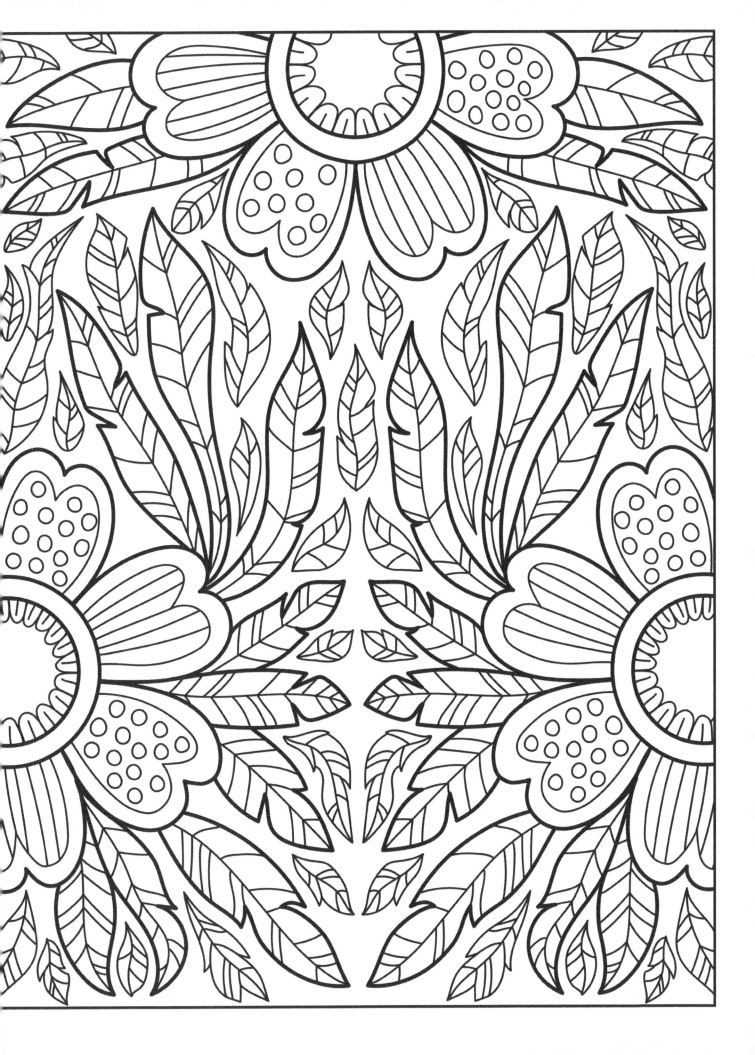

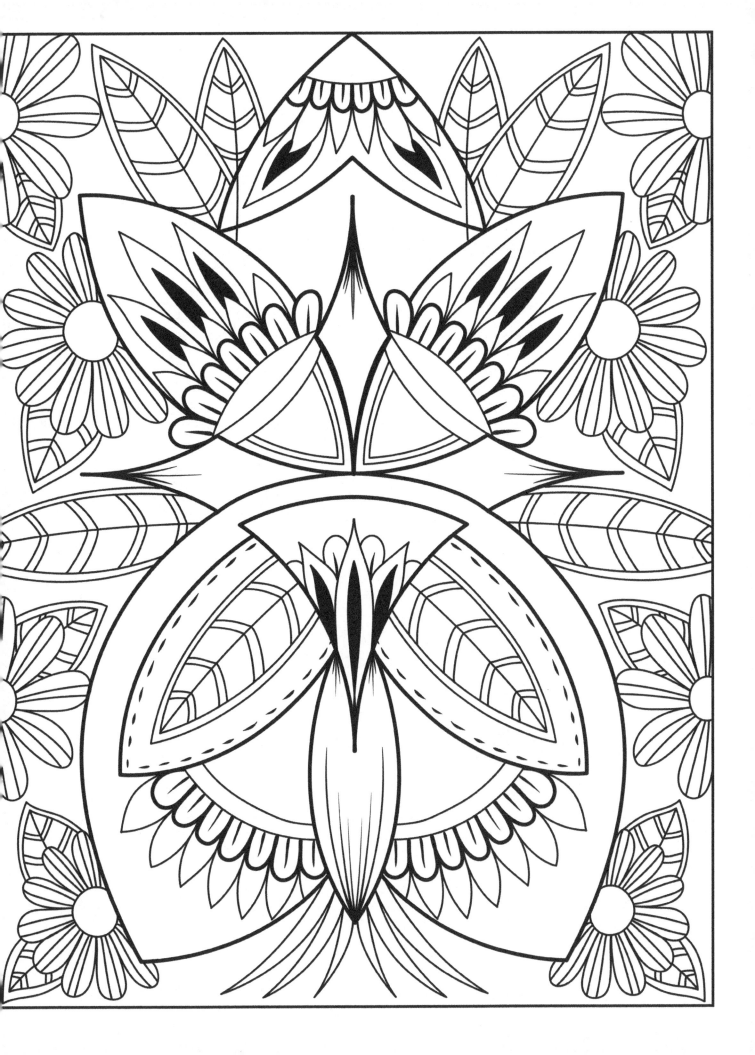

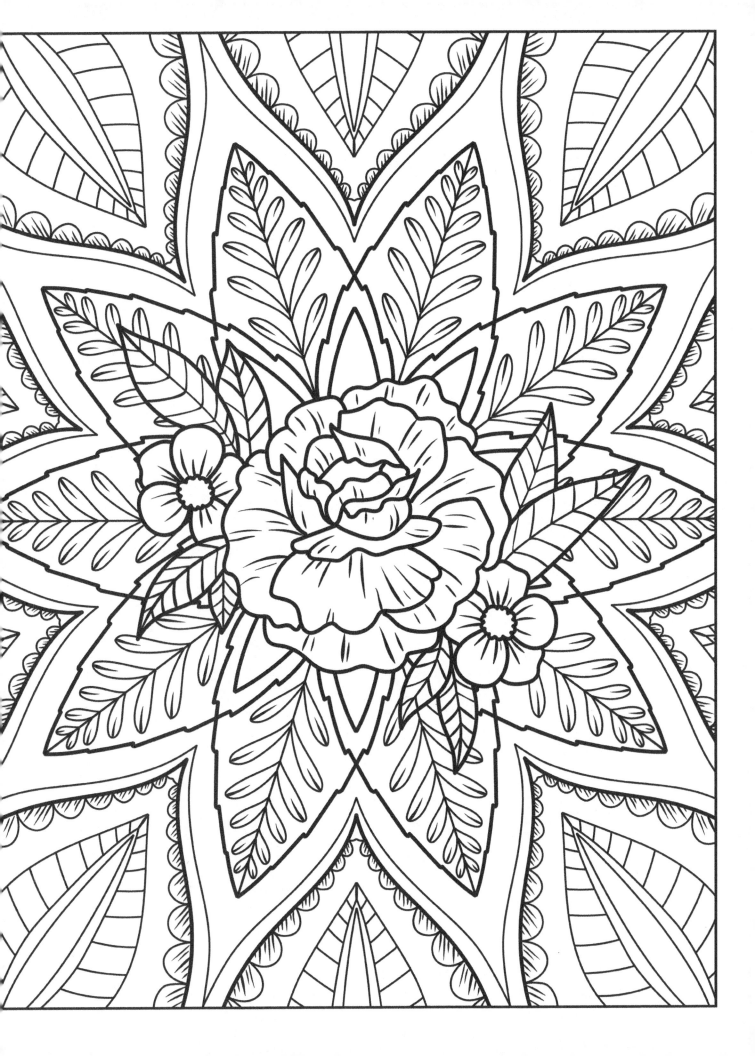

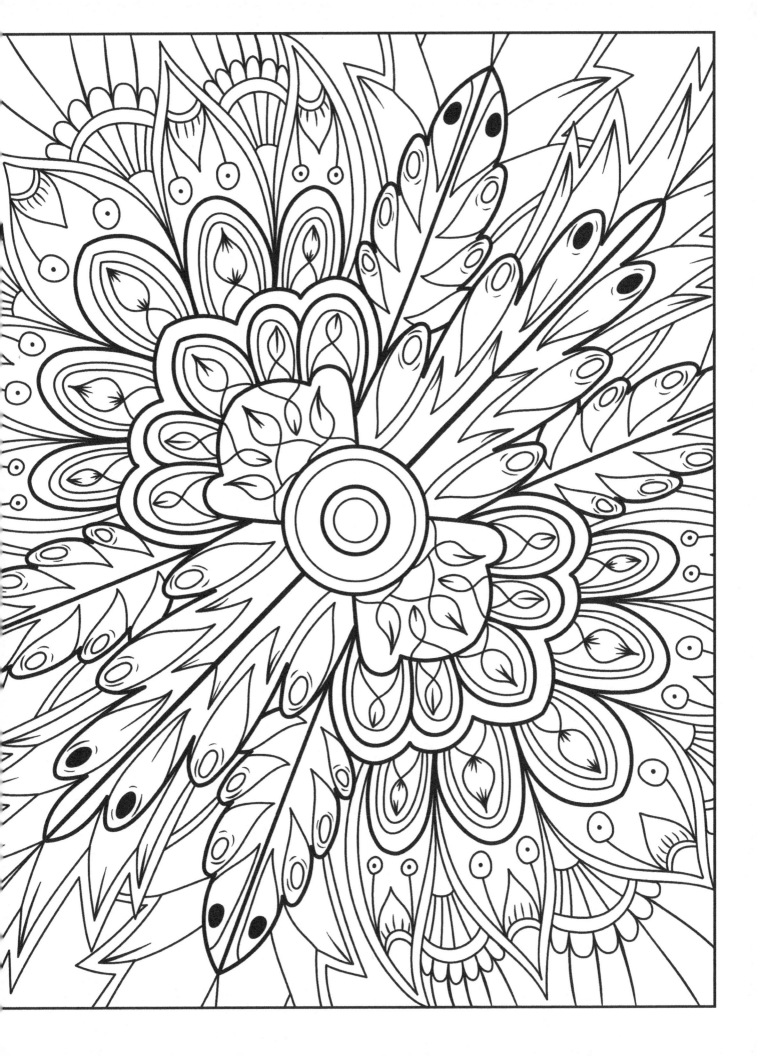

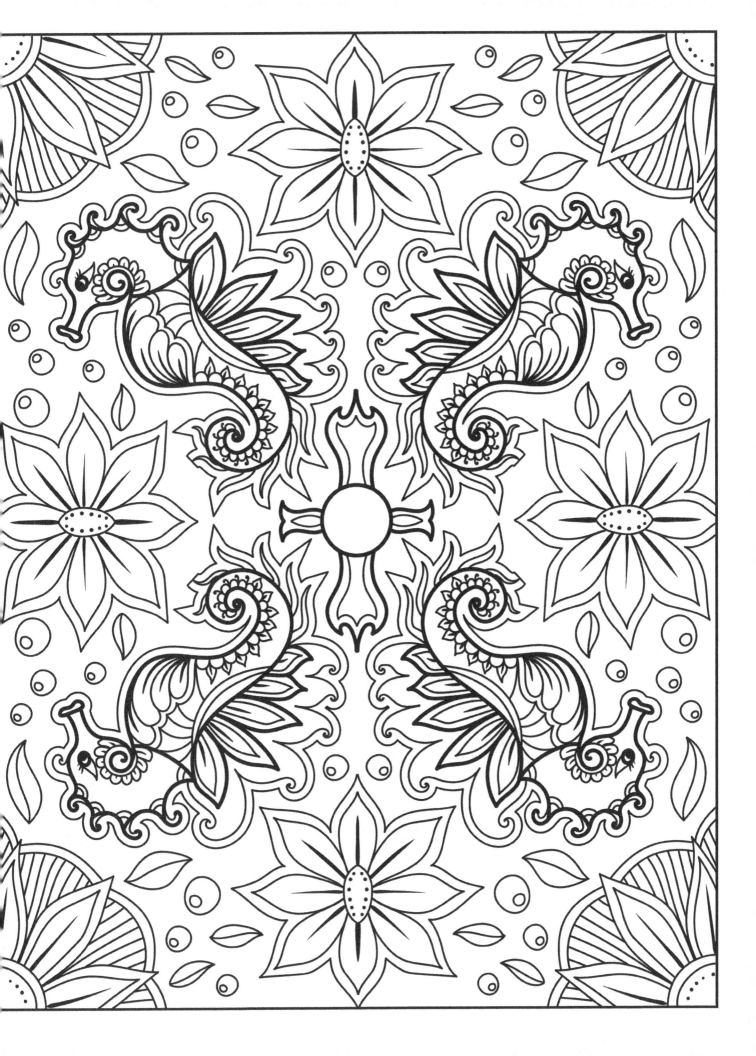

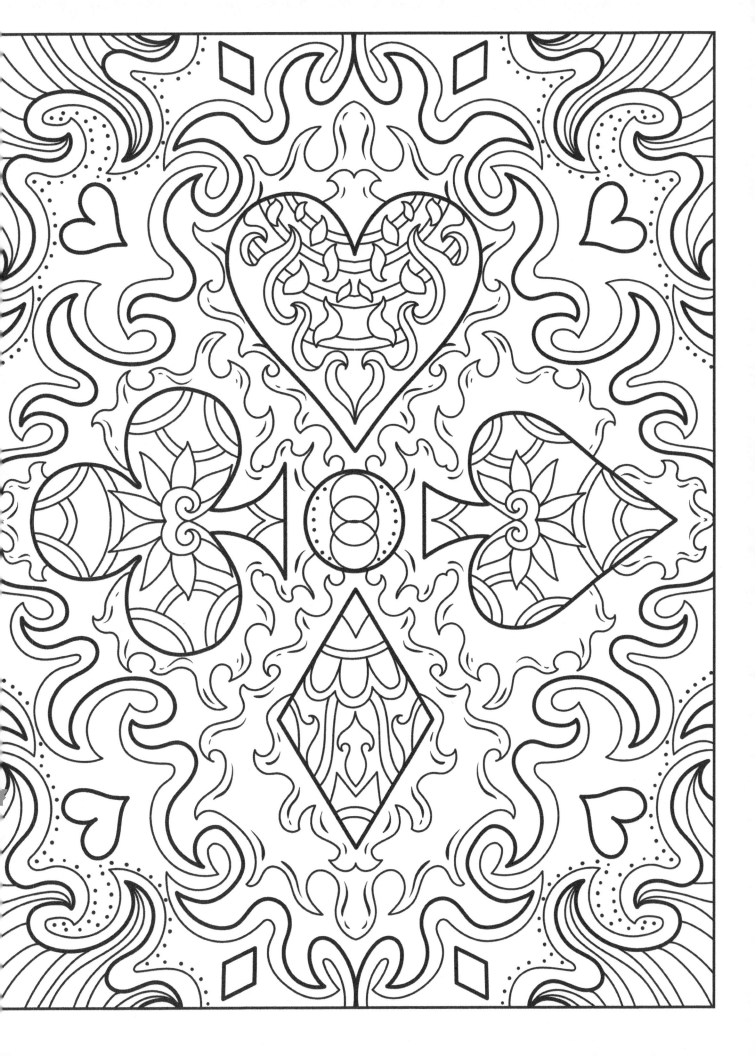

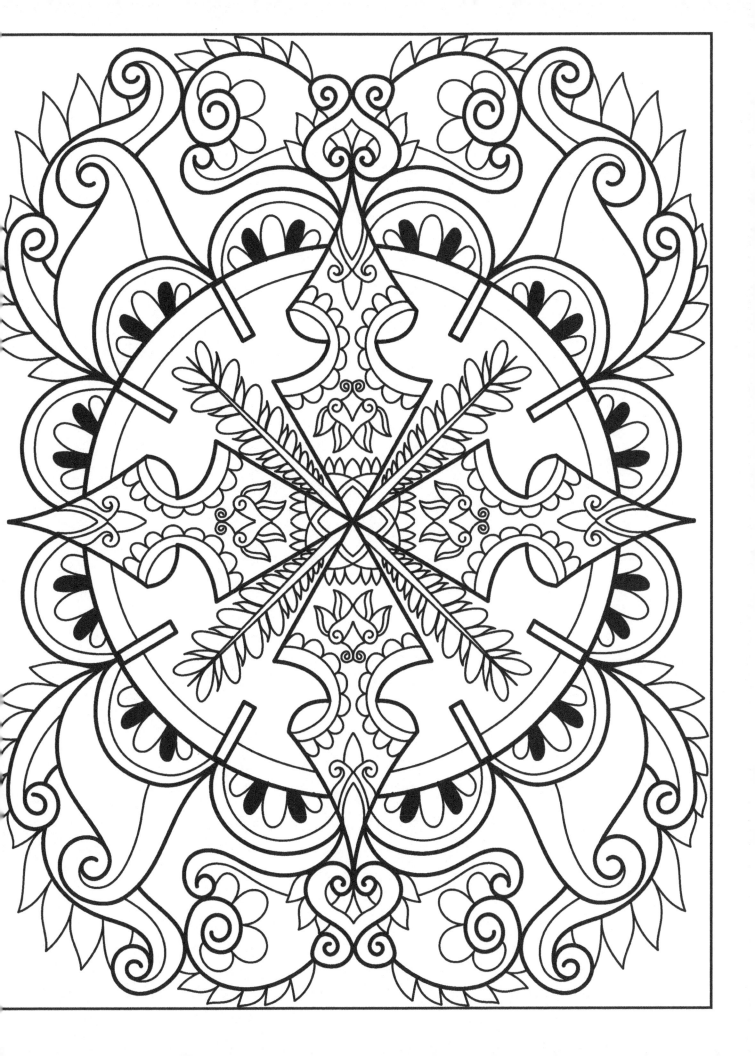

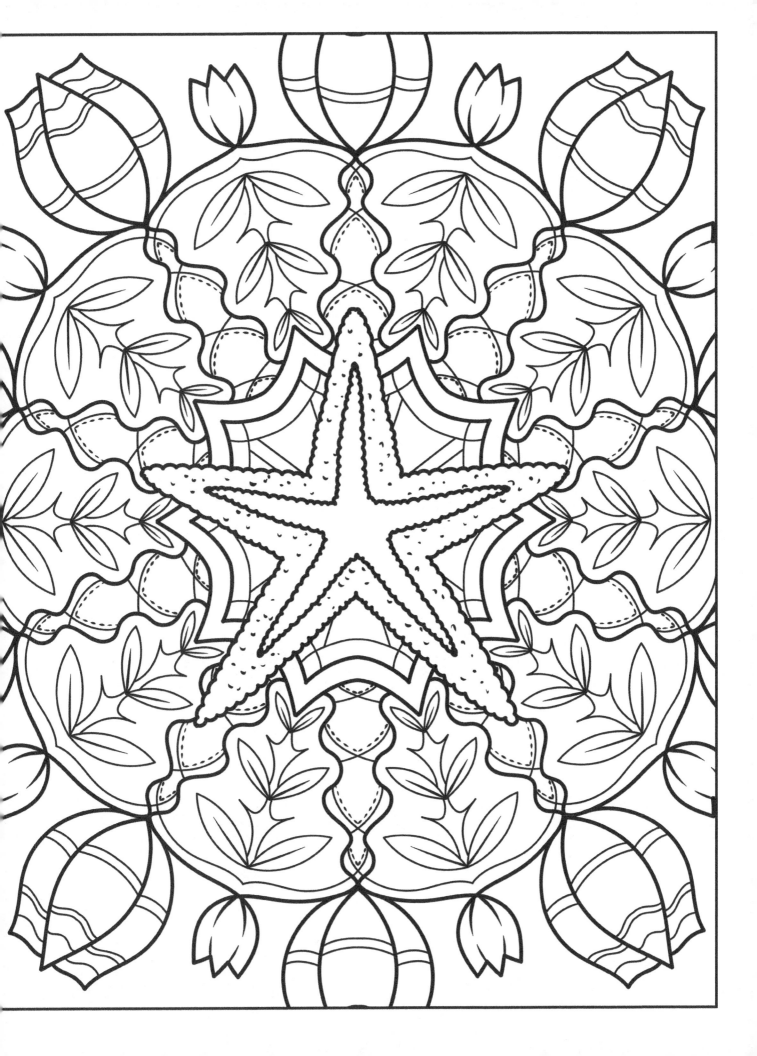

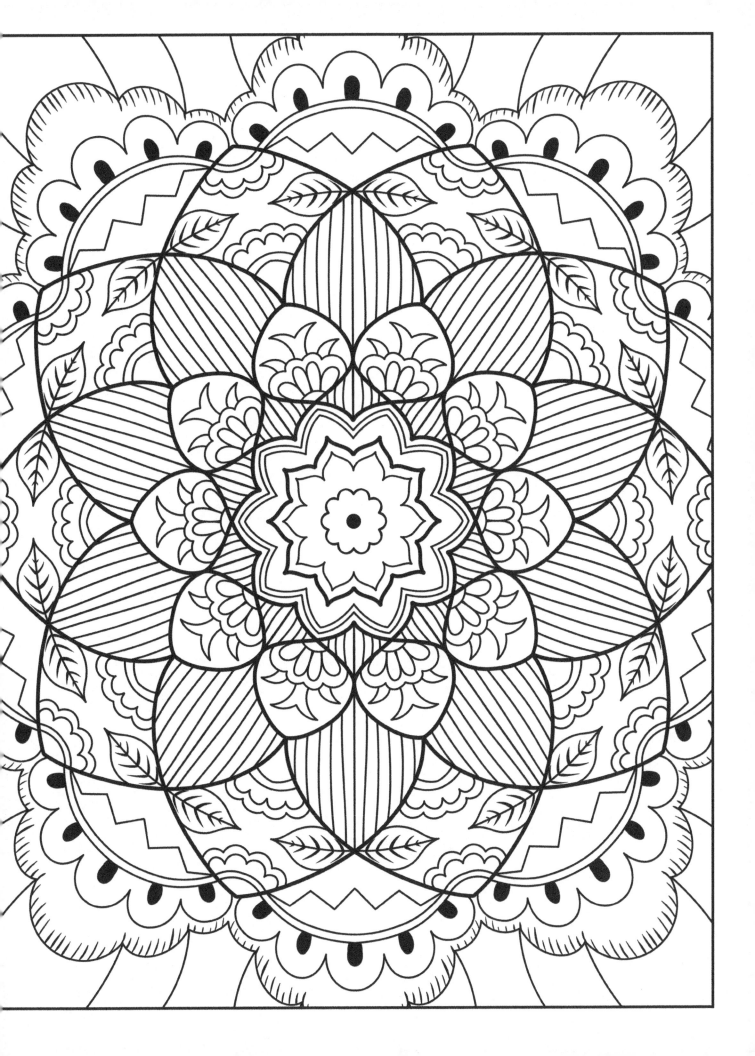

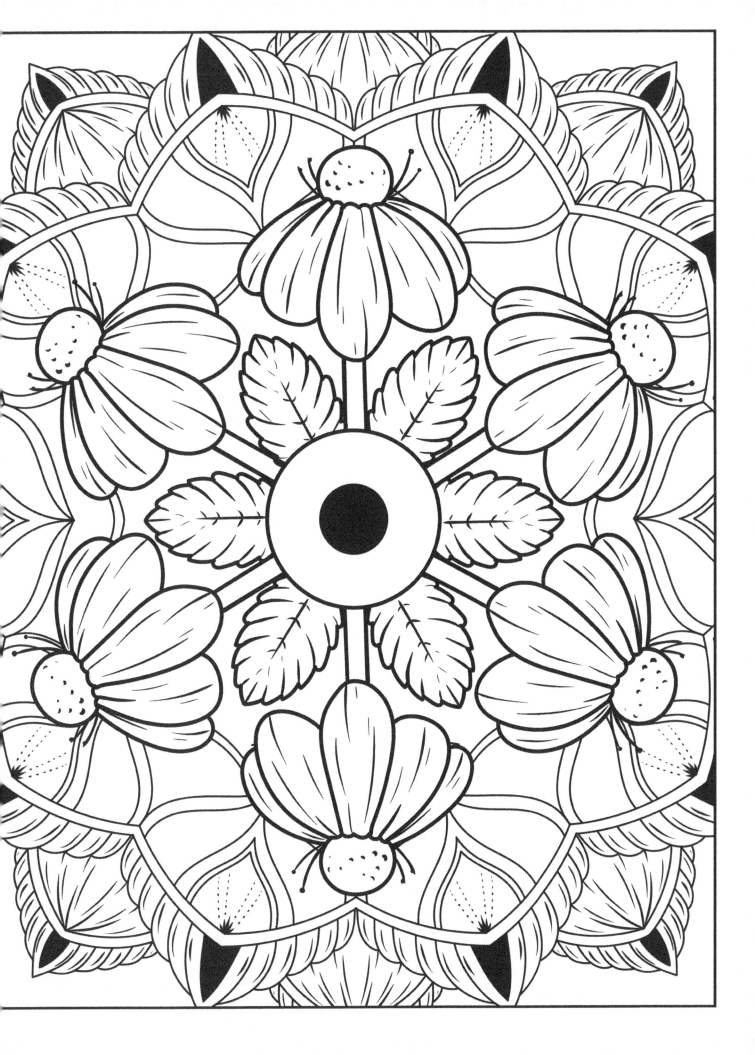

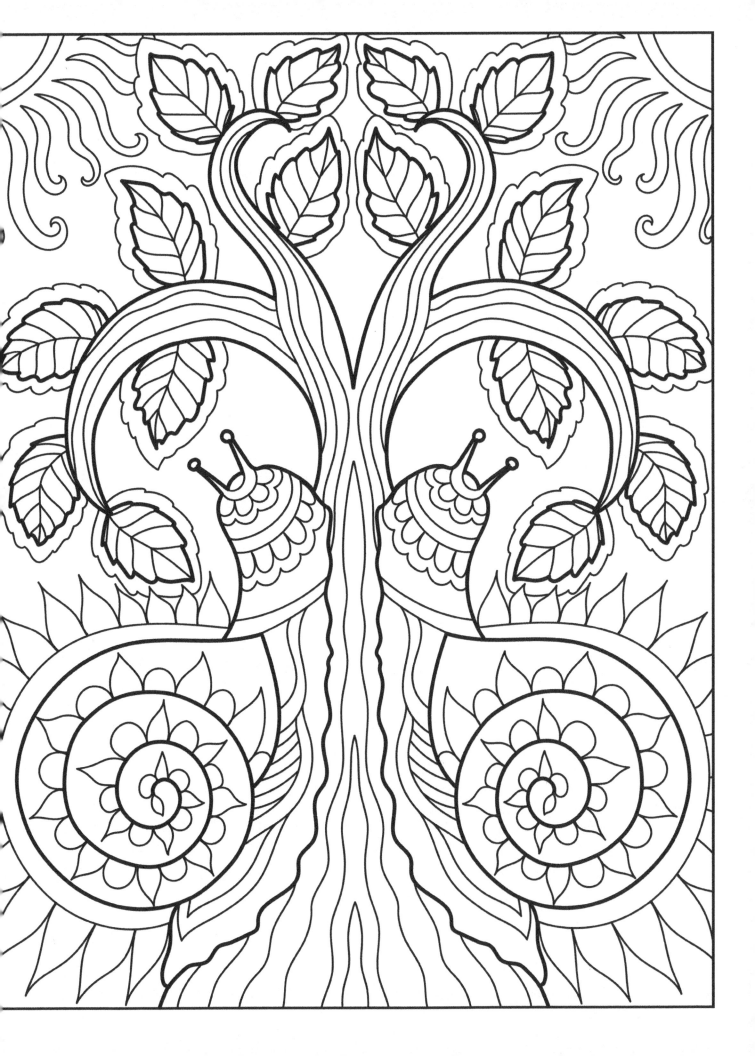

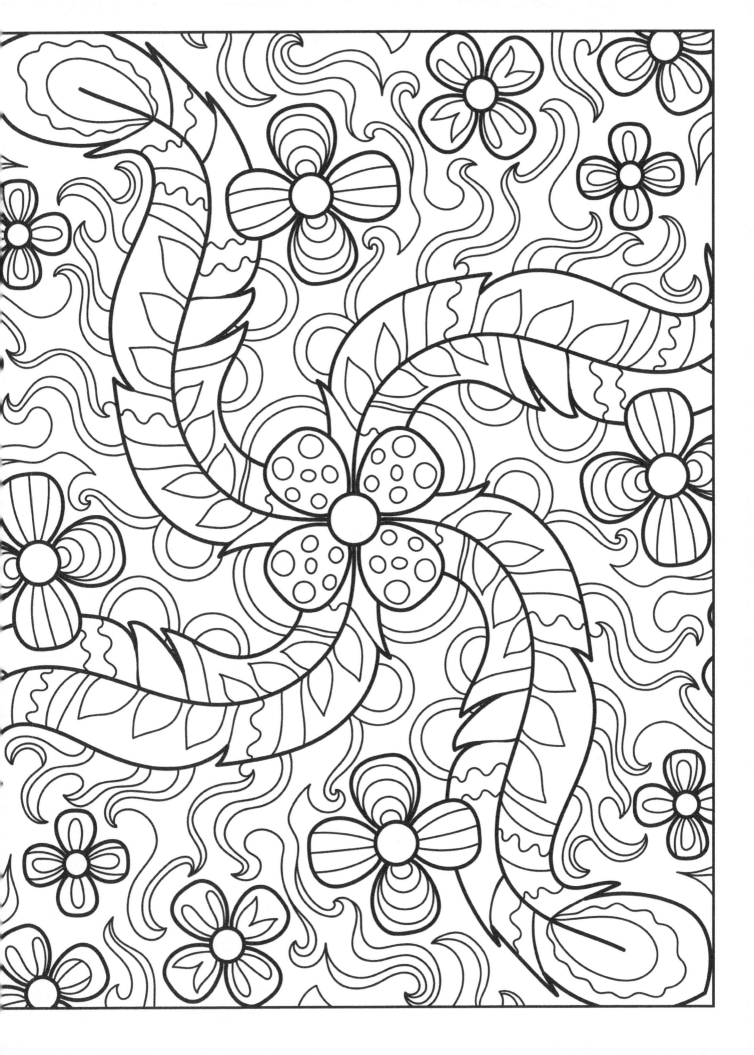

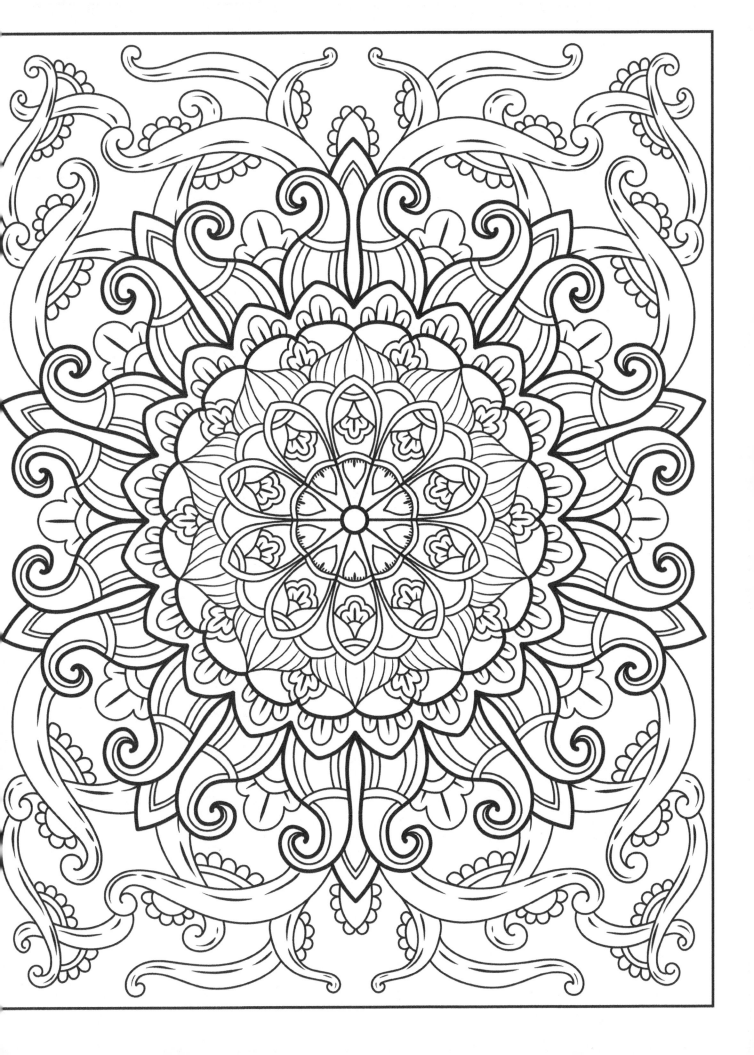

Jeanettveronicastudio

If you enjoyed my Coloring Book please consider leaving a review. It means the world to me.

With Coffee and Love,
Jeanett Veronica

Find all my coloring books
on Amazon:

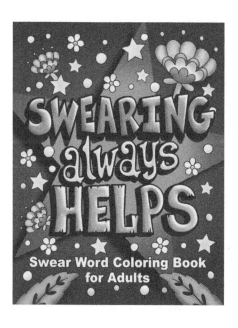

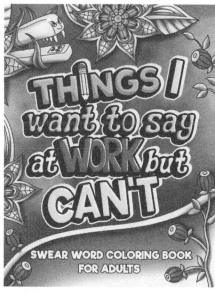

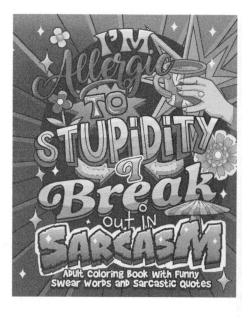

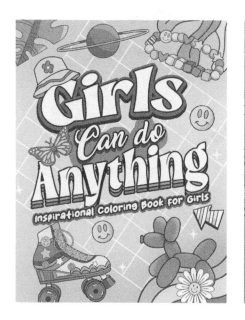

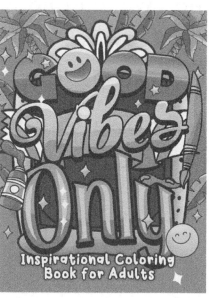

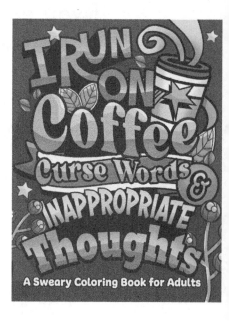